Colour in the Garden

Val Bourne

Colour
in the
Garden

MERRELL
LONDON · NEW YORK

Contents

Introduction

I grew up in a sepia age of beige and brown. At a time when every child had to emulate Princess Anne or Prince Charles, I was dressed in brown Harris tweed and sensible button-up shoes, and even my socks were fawn. The hall at home had brown paintwork and cream Anaglypta wallpaper; photos came in black and white; and the most exciting things were cocoa and the glow from the radio.

My release was a weekend infusion of real colour supplied by a multitude of Punjabi ladies, whom I encountered shopping on my local high street, saried, glowing and bejewelled from nose to toe. I drank in every detail and followed every movement of their billowing saris as they tossed them back and forth over one shoulder with all the style of Bollywood actresses. The soft, swirling fabric was often separated by a bare, brown middle, which made the sequinned emerald greens, bright pinks and pastel blues even more exotic and colourful to a child dressed in neutrals.

I knew then that I had to have colour, and, although I would have preferred toe jewellery, nail varnish and a crimson sari, I chose flowers instead. While other teenagers I knew were out at night at discos, I was tucked up in bed with plant catalogues or constructing begging letters to botanic gardens around the world, in search of some treasure or other. It was the start of a lifetime of growing plants.

I didn't realize it at the time, but the shades of those Indian silks and cottons, which were literally a bolt from the blue, affected my mood. They lifted my spirits and the sun

Hordeum jubatum, an annual grass easily grown in a warm position, frames the stately, stiff-stemmed *Achillea* 'Terracotta'. By high summer the colours of this long-term planting combination will have faded to biscuit and beige.

came out inside my head. That is the thing about colour: it changes your mood and makes you feel calmer, or more excited, or more romantic.

The effect is a purely personal one, however, and this book, although it offers tried-and-tested seasonal plant recipes, is not meant to be prescriptive. Please experiment creatively. Being prescriptive is bad news, as I discovered more than thirty years ago when I went to visit a garden with completely blue-themed borders. It was a weekend opening in June, and I went alone on a bright Saturday and thought it splendid. When Sunday dawned the weather was grey, flat and uninspiring and so were the borders, as lifeless and bland as day-old Yorkshire pudding. My companion, who was expecting so much, was clearly disappointed. That showed me how light affects colour, and that a good border has to be robust enough in colour and form to look good in both gloom and bright light. Monochrome schemes (perhaps with the exception of white borders enclosed by yew) rarely work.

Changes in light occur naturally throughout the year in countries that are blessed with seasonal weather. As the Earth's axis tilts, the sun's position in the sky changes. In winter in the northern hemisphere the sun is at its lowest point, and it backlights the garden, picking up detail and strengthening colours. The one constant is that we are as powerless as King Canute, because we can't command the weather.

In summer the sun is directly overhead. This brighter light tends to wash colour out, so the garden appears to be full of

Spring zing at its best,
with *Allium hollandicum*
'Purple Sensation' and
Euphorbia palustris.

pastels, rather like a watercolour painting. However, if we could freeze-frame the borders until September, or pickle them in aspic, those same plants would look vibrant and colourful under the crisper autumnal light. September makes every flower look like a jewel: it's the best light in the gardening year in the northern hemisphere.

Although seasonal changes in light are useful, gardeners should cast some of their own shade to create a magic-lantern pattern of moving light in their gardens. The easiest way is to plant small, ornamental trees with airy canopies. It could be choice white-stemmed Himalayan birches, such as *Betula utilis* var. *jacquemontii* 'Doorenbos' or *B. utilis* var. *jacquemontii* 'Grayswood Ghost', or the Tibetan cherry (*Prunus serrula*), or, if your drainage is good enough, an ornamental rowan, such as *Sorbus* 'Pink Pagoda'. Then, when the sunlight slants through the canopy as the Earth moves round the Sun, dappled patches of light and shade appear on the ground in your garden, and change through the day. This is much more flattering than open, stark light, and you can use the dappled shade for spring-flowering opportunists, which nip in just before the leafy canopy closes overhead. They will be sheltered by the benign branches and soil-warming, moisture-absorbing roots.

Small ornamental trees also give a sense of scale to lesser herbaceous planting. Oriental hellebores, for instance, look much better if they are close to an ornamental tree that flowers at the same time; on their own, they simply form a carpet across the ground. I use three blossoming trees that flower when the wood is bare. *Prunus* 'Kursar' produces bright-pink flowers from downwards-facing buds in mid-spring, but this small tree usually shows a glint of pink as the buds split in February. The foliage eventually joins in with the flowers. The winter-flowering cherry, *P. × subhirtella* 'Autumnalis', provides spidery dark branches and confetti-like petals in flourishes between November and March. The Japanese apricot, *P. mume* 'Beni-chidori', has vivid flowers in rose madder, but only after a warm summer.

Combining Plants: The Three-Month Border

Learning how to combine colours to good effect in the garden is much more difficult than simply putting together a colour-themed outfit for a wedding, for instance, or decorating a room, because flowers are ephemeral – they come and go. The

The best metallic plant sculpture of all is the branching silver-stemmed biennial *Eryngium giganteum*.

bitter truth is that your chosen plants have to flower at the same time as well as complementing each other visually: it is no good combining an August-flowering dahlia with a June-flowering campanula, however flattering they might be in theory, for they will be like ships that pass in the night. Your chosen plants must peak together reliably year after year.

With that in mind, experience has taught me the benefit of a three-month border, which contains a similar range of plants that flower within that time. Once the flowers have faded the foliage and possibly seed heads will remain, so the season of interest extends beyond the flowering time.

This does not mean that your three-month border should begin or end sharply. The trick is to extend it by adding earlier- and later-flowering plants. My rose and peony borders peak in May and June, but linger until November with the help of pink and white annual daisies (*Cosmos bipinnatus*), the trembling blush-white wands of *Gaura lindheimeri*, black and white annual scabious (from seed mixes containing *Scabiosa atropurpurea*), remontant (repeat-flowering) hardy geraniums, such as 'Orion', and any other plants I can persuade to keep flowering by judicious deadheading. If the summer is warm enough, the wonderfully glamorous (but lethally spiny) *Cleome hassleriana* also adds a presence: it's one of the best follow-up acts for roses. The backbone planting, however, is all May and June – rather blowsy and Edwardian – and my extension planting is also soft and feminine, reflecting the same peony shades of pink. Earlier planting in this scheme is a mixture of varieties of *Viola cornuta* (a truly perennial viola, with elegantly winged flowers in shades of white, blue and mauve) with *Heuchera*, × *Heucherella* and refined forms of London Pride: *Saxifraga* × *urbium* 'Miss Chambers' and one sold as S. × *geum* Dixter form. This area of my garden is also packed with a variety of tulips.

If you devote the hottest, sunniest, driest part of your garden to summer-flowering plants, many of them are likely to have silvered, aromatic foliage. This on its own will create harmony, and it will lead you towards cooler purples, mauves, pinks and blues. This area is also perfect for later-flowering shrubby salvias (varieties of S. *microphylla* and S. *greggii* and their naturally occurring hybrid S. × *jamensis*) and penstemons, which will perform late into the year, glowing against the silver foliage.

Shade can be equally beguiling, and spring-flowering woodlanders and bulbs flourish on the

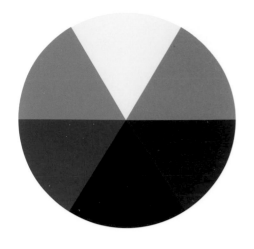

A simple colour wheel.

quieter edges of the garden. They are often persuaded into precocious flower by the presence of overhead trees and shrubs. Shade is also perfect for uplifting golden foliage (which scorches in full sun) and good, green evergreens, both of which look more luscious out of full sun.

Position your autumn-flowering plants where warm afternoon sunshine falls in order to keep the butterflies happy, because late-summer and autumn nectar flows in warm conditions. The daisy dominates this season, with golden and pallid yellows, rusty oranges and lots of mauve-pinks. Often the central discs of daisies are burnished and bronzed, and this mutual colour allows them to mingle effectively without creating a clash between pink and yellow. But the autumn border can also move and sway with taller grasses, spikes, spires and such tender plants as dahlias. There's a decadent air to autumn, and this is when dahlias (surely the most colourful and explosive plant in the garden) look their best.

By developing and extending three-month borders you will be adopting the 'right plant in the right place' philosophy, and this will ensure that your planting schemes work practically. You may have to tailor your choices to suit your conditions, though. If you have a dry garden with less than 50 centimetres (20 in.) of rainfall a year, leave the moisture-loving plants (such as ligularias, astilbes, phloxes and hostas) to those who garden in wetter parts, and develop a taste for steely eryngiums, dianthus, silvered sages, delicate yellow anthemis and filigree-leafed achilleas instead.

Understanding How Colour Works

It is important to understand how colours work together. Although most gardeners start by creating a glorious jumble of different colours, this soon loses its appeal, because such gardens are restless affairs that jar the eye and the spirit. The next stage is trying to combine colours by selecting plants.

Light colours (left to right: *Viola cornuta*, *Cosmos bipinnatus*, a pink daphne and *Nicotiana* 'Lime Green').

Dark colours (left to right: *Rudbeckia fulgida* var. *sullivantii* 'Goldsturm', *Kniphofia uvaria* 'Nobilis', *Geranium ibericum* and *Agapanthus caulescens*).

At this point it is worth examining colour theory by looking at a six-part colour wheel that shows the three primary colours (red, blue and yellow) with the three secondaries (orange, green and purple) between them (see opposite).

These six colours are ranged in a wheel, and once more shades are added there is a warm half and a cool half. The dividing line cuts through the reds at one end and the greens at the other. The reds with more purple in them are cool, while those with more orange are warmer and sunnier. The greens with more yellow are warmer and those with more blue are cool. Colours opposite each other on the colour wheel are complementary. When placed side by side they make a dynamic combination because both colours look more vibrant. Good examples are red and green, blue and yellow, and green and purple. These combinations dazzle the eye but remain pleasant. Choosing three adjacent colours on the wheel (such as orange, yellow and red, or pink, purple and blue) forms a blend and creates visual harmony. It's relaxing and pleasing, and the colours look as if they belong together – as indeed they do.

In theory we could find a plant to match every shade in the colour wheel. The trouble is – and this is the nitty-gritty – that certain colours are much more in evidence at certain times of the year. The chances are that all the sunshine-yellows you want to grow in the perennial line are either late-summer- or autumn-flowering daisies. The oranges tend to be late-summer red-hot pokers and crocosmias, and the few true-blue plants on offer are mostly tender Mexican salvias or South African agapanthus, also from late summer.

In other words, there is a natural palette of colour that changes through the year along with the light levels, since the height of the sun affects our perception of colour. Certain groups of plants dominate certain seasons. Woodlanders tend to dominate spring, while late June is the best time for all roses because the once-and-only-flowering varieties are in full flow.

Winter flowers – snowdrops, *Lonicera × purpusii* 'Winter Beauty' and *Daphne bholua* 'Jacqueline Postill', for example – tend to be small, subtle and sometimes scented. They make an impact against the low skies and bare earth, but they are quiet performers and would be lost in summer sunshine. Between March and mid-May a plethora of spring bulbs are available to the gardener, and the clear light of spring sharpens their bright colours. This is a season for discernment, and some gardeners will happily champion the brightest yellow daffodils, while others go for pale yellow and white.

From mid-May onwards soft-green foliage abounds, and this is one time when white flowers look cool and elegant. The light is still gentle enough to capture the subtleties of ruffed astrantias, such as *A. major* subsp. *involucrata* 'Shaggy', or to pick up the green shading on *Tulipa* 'Spring Green' when it's hidden in the gloomy depths. By June, however, the green-eyed white rose, *Rosa* 'Madame Hardy', looks far too icy and remote among the summer froth. Summer demands softer blush-whites.

The overhead sun of summer dilutes colours, but the natural palette of this season tends to be softer anyway, with blue and silver-pink campanulas, lavender, fringed pinks, silvered alliums, hardy geraniums and hardy salvias. However, there's plenty of scope for making a statement with something like the postbox-red oriental poppy *Papaver orientale* 'Beauty of Livermere'.

In autumn, light levels lower to deepen colours, but that does not explain the jewel-box effect completely. By now tender plants from the southern hemisphere (including

A purple and red border with astrantia, salvia, valerian and cimicifuga.

dahlias, colourful salvias and penstemons) are in full flowering mode and their flowers have much more pigment in their petals, preventing sun scorch. Tender cannas and hedychiums have been persuaded into flower, and the prairie plants (heleniums, echinaceas and asters) are either still blooming or about to flower.

Close examination of a flower always reveals a helpful detail, a clue to what could go where. The pink potentilla with orange stamens and a rusty middle could jostle quite happily with an orange flower, although the first thought would be 'No!' The purple-eyed white verbascum (the truly perennial *V. chaixii* 'Album') is a wonderful foil for moody purple or red roses and sombre maroons. The purple-veined *Geranium clarkei* 'Kashmir White' will pick up any blues and purples. The yellow middle of an aster will mix with strong yellows, or pick up the tones of orange dahlias and crocosmias. Always examine the veining, the stamens, the style and the central disc, and observe the buds and leaves.

Never discount foliage. Mixing the scalloped leaves of *Heuchera* 'Tiramisu' (its shawl-shaped golden foliage mottled in brick-red with a cool hint of chartreuse) with the all-gold version of the ever-moving and curtseying Hakon grass (*Hakonechloa macra* 'All Gold') against a dainty, spidery orange-flowered epimedium, such as 'Amber Queen', will delight the eye from April until late in the year, not least because many epimediums have heart-shaped, veined foliage.

Although these two reds are very different in tone, from the scarlet *Dahlia* 'Bishop of Llandaff' to the berry-coloured *Achillea millefolium* 'Red Velvet', the colours blend thanks to the golden awns of *Stipa gigantea*.

Planning Your Planting

Too many gardeners focus on the fleeting flowers rather than the stems, buds and leaves. Plants come as a package, and most make a contribution to a border for weeks before and after they flower. I find the following four indispensable in that respect, and they mingle beautifully. *Origanum laevigatum* 'Herrenhausen' has tight rosettes of crinkled foliage early in the year, and these look almost black against the bare earth. Then the stems extend and the flower buds develop so that each one looks like a miniature black cauliflower on a stalk. Gradually, by August, the dark-purple calices release their lighter mauve-pink flowers, much to the delight of Small Tortoiseshell butterflies and common carder bees (*Bombus pascuorum*). As autumn wends its way towards winter, the black lacy seed head endures like a spaced-out sea lavender. *Aster divaricatus* (a favourite of Gertrude Jekyll) has small white starry flowers and it flops, which is not an inspiring thought. However, the stems weave and bend as they do so, and these wiry, shiny stems are ebony against the diamond-shaped emerald leaves. As the flowers appear the foliage darkens to dusky purple, picking up the colour of 'Herrenhausen' and a compact umbellifer with muddy-purple buds: *Seseli hippomarathrum*. This also catches the eye long before it flowers, for its tiny inch-wide heads are delicate green pincushions and they wave above the bright-green ferny foliage. Finally, *Anemone hupehensis* var. *japonica* 'Pamina' (a bright-pink, neatly frilled Japanese anemone) rises up to produce pearl-like buds in soft grey, a long time before it flowers. Needless to say, all four are repeated along my border.

Don't let your garden grow like Topsy; try to plan, and when planning aim to choose the best plants you can find for your chosen colour scheme. The best way to achieve this is to buy a Royal Horticultural Society (RHS) *Plant Finder* or look at the RHS website under 'Plants', and identify the Award of Garden Merit (AGM) winners by the cup logo printed beside their names. The AGM is awarded to plants that have outshone their rivals on the trial field for a period of three years. They have been judged by experts for garden-worthiness and are the very best in their genus. Then find out where you can buy them. Nurserymen will advise, but many don't garden. They grow plants in pots and that is a very different thing.

When ordering your plants, go to a good mail-order nursery so that you can acquire the right number of each

A river of blue muscari
shows off a variety of
yellow daffodils perfectly.

plant. One is not enough, sadly. You must learn to restrict the number of different plants you grow, but grow more of each one. The best gardens contain swathes of planting, and that might mean buying in threes, fives, sevens or nines depending on the size of your border (odd numbers always work best). Weave them through your border in a ribbon, which usually looks much more natural than a blobby block or a straight line.

Identify the flowering time of each variety, then choose a plant to accompany it with the aim of mixing textures. If you chose a daisy first, go for a spire, or a flat-topped flower, or a grass. This avoids the rumpled duvet look, because the most important constituent of any border is the vertical accents, which take the eye to the sky and break the monopoly of mounds. It needn't be flowers; the spiky foliage of kniphofias, crocosmias and hemerocallis can serve the same purpose.

Finally, once you've planted your scheme, keep a notebook with sections for each part of your garden. Note the successes and failures. Exercise your ruthless streak and change any dodgy combinations; if you chose good plants they will almost certainly be useful somewhere else.

At the same time, buy another notebook for garden visiting. Visit good gardens in your area, ones that should

share your soil type and climate. Look for good plant combinations and write them down. Try to experience successful gardens, venturing out to the best ones you can get to. Look for an excellent nursery and plunder it regularly for ideas.

This book is divided into seasons, and each contains three 'colour recipes' that really work at that time of year. You won't have to struggle to find plants to use. The combinations will succeed without any contrivance: nothing is forced into flower early, or held back, and plants are not plunged downwards or raised up (all techniques that are sometimes employed by designers of show gardens at major flower shows, resulting in totally impracticable combinations that make me sigh). My combinations do work, and the plants chosen are the best in their field. I've spent decades growing plants and ditching the poor performers; you have to kiss a lot of frogs in gardening before you find your princes. More importantly, the colour combinations work in the conditions and light provided by that particular season. The result is that you can use every part of your garden to full advantage and always have something to admire.

Spring Zing

*Emulate the energy of spring with lime greens
and fluorescent acid-yellows set against mauves,
purples and blues.*

Spring is the most exuberant season of all, and the colour
that captures this energy better than any other is polychrome
yellow – the sort that has built-in luminescence. One plant is
indispensable when it comes to radiating this sort of bright
spring zing: the euphorbia, or spurge. The flower structure
of rounded papery bracts protecting a tiny star-like bloom
ensures that each flower has a long-lasting presence and may
give two months' value. The flowers are either packed on a
crozier (as E. × *martini*) or arranged in a flat umbel-like head.
Some varieties also have cyathium leaves (false flowers) and
the most spectacular example is the poinsettia (E. *pulcherrima*)
with its red ruff. In many euphorbias the leaves at the top of
the flowering stem are attractively coloured, increasing their
impact. The downside is that care must always be taken when
cutting or handling euphorbias because the white latex-like
sap (which shows that they are related to plants used in the
production of rubber) is an irritant. It will give you a rash and
can damage your eyes, and as you cut, it runs freely. Wearing

Euphorbia polychroma.

Euphorbia amygdaloides
var. robbiae.

goggles and long sleeves is advisable, and this isn't health-and-safety nonsense – it's self-preservation.

Some of the best euphorbias for early spring zing have bonny rosettes of evergreen foliage that persists through the winter. To keep these evergreen euphorbias in good heart, cut the old stems back to the base once you see new growth (technically known as basal shoots) emerging. This yearly summer trim will greatly lengthen the life of your plants. Cuttings (from the new basal shoots) should be taken every year if possible, because evergreen euphorbias tend to lose vigour and need replacing very third or fourth year. Cuttings are easy: slice off the new growth when it reaches 7.5 centimetres (3 in.), strip off the lower leaves and plunge the cutting into a suitable medium (half and half sand and compost is ideal). Pot up in compost once rooted.

The deciduous euphorbias, which die away in winter, tend to be longer-lived and can be propagated by division in autumn or cuttings in spring. Some produce asparagus-like spears in April, and these can be a feature in themselves; the glassy cerise-pink stems of E. sikkimensis, for example, are legendary. Their most flattering bedfellows colour-wise are equally strong blues and purples, and both colours abound in spring. This makes the show exciting. But you could also use greens, creams and oranges to make a more restful border – although a splash of purple would always be the cherry on the cake.

The euphorbia that delivers the best clean-yellow glare is undoubtedly the aptly named E. polychroma, which by March forms a pouffe of flowering stems about 60 centimetres (2 ft) high. It's not fussy about soil, but it does best (and looks best, too) in dappled shade. Forms vary, but I have trawled through plenty and come to the conclusion that the finest is 'Golden Fusion' because the flowering stems are packed together in a pleasing way, giving maximum eye appeal. The cyathium leaves are large and cup-forming, and the effects last until June. The relatively low height makes this plant a perfect partner for miniature spring-flowering bulbs, particularly muscari and scilla, although a deep-purple crocus (such as the March-flowering C. vernus 'Remembrance') would also work brilliantly. Scilla siberica, or the spring squill – a superstar with its cobalt-blue pendent bells – could be left to self-seed. The named form 'Spring Beauty' is said by discerning bulb-growers to be darker, stronger and more robust. Snap it up if you see it; it's the only scilla I would use. S. bifolia is a duller blue and has the largest testicle-like seed heads, with several pods per stem. These do need removing before they leave you with thousands of grass-like seedlings.

Any blue muscari would work, too, but some are thugs, hell-bent on taking over the entire garden – with ugly foliage thrown in. I recommend *M. latifolium*, a beefy grape hyacinth with two-tone navy bells at the base and a pale-blue top, with tulip-like leaves. *M. azureum* has that touch of summer blue in a plump head that seems to stay in bud for months, and *M. armeniacum* 'Valerie Finnis' is a Cambridge blue with a hint of cool green. She often flowers later. There are also deep-blue doubles, including 'Blue Spike'.

Your dark glint of blue and purple could equally well come from a pulmonaria called 'Diana Clare', the one I rate most highly. It combines silvered foliage in the verdigris tone of

weathered copper roofs with heads of deep-violet flowers.
'Blue Ensign' is also superb, and is interesting from the
moment it creeps up through the ground in early spring,
showing purple-tinted dark shoots that become linear green
leaves teamed with tight heads of gentian-blue flowers.

Other gleams of clear yellow can be tucked away in deeper
shade. Two smyrniums will do the trick for you. The most
beguiling is S. *perfoliatum*, but it's also the most difficult
because it's a biennial. It will self-seed moderately, if left to its
own devices, giving you one year on and one year off, but be
warned: you'll have no joy collecting and sowing the seeds in
a pot. Buy three plants one year and three the next, then let
them get on with it, and with luck every year you will have
a glimmer of gold provided by bright-yellow umbels clasped
by equally bright-yellow foliage. S. *rotundifolium* is a perennial
with stout branching stems topped by bright-yellow flowers.
It also produces lots of shiny black seeds, but there the
resemblance with the lovely biennial ends. S. *rotundifolium*
is an ugly sister, as graceful as a mobile-telephone mast
masquerading as a tree. The ultimate addition to this border is
a sprinkling of purple-blue spurred aquilegias and perhaps a
golden hop (*Humulus lupulus* 'Aureus') climbing a wall or fence.

The name of plantsman E.A. Bowles is associated with
two yellow grass-like plants that are British natives. One is a
sedge discovered on Wicken Fen in Cambridgeshire, and that
should indicate that *Carex elata* 'Aurea' (commonly known
as Bowles's golden sedge) needs good, moist soil in order to
produce its soft fountain of green-edged, cool-yellow leaves.
If you can grow it, the brown caterpillar-like flowers are a
wonderful foil for the foliage. Easier by far is a self-seeding
evergreen millet, *Milium effusum* 'Aureum' (Bowles's golden
grass). The leaves keep a bright colour over winter, but they
splay awkwardly so have limited charm. However, all is
forgiven once they flower in early May and display finely
beaded yellow awns that shine in full sun. There is a named
form, 'Yaffle', but there seems to be little difference. You
could also try a golden luzula (*L. sylvatica* 'Aurea') for its loose
arrangement of wide leaves (like a golden spider plant), which
look stunning against the bare earth of early spring.

Euphorbia polychroma is a tight clump-former that stays
put. However, there are other spring-zing euphorbias with a
wandering habit. One – E. *cyparissias* – should (in my opinion)
never be planted in a garden unless it's in a wild border
of thuggish plants. Romantically called the ploughboy's
mignonette, this foot-high feathery euphorbia with round
heads of yellow flowers looks well behaved enough from
above the ground, but let it loose and the word rampant

would fail to come close. A red-topped form, 'Fens Ruby', is no better. Plant it to your cost, unless – like Gertrude Jekyll – you have a huge woodland garden.

More well behaved is a euphorbia grown for many years under the name of Mrs Robb, a formidable Victorian who carried it home from Turkey in her hatbox. This lady, on a 'mini' grand tour, spotted a spreading euphorbia on a hillside from the stagecoach window. She had the presence of mind to stop the coach, gather up a section (not to be recommended today) and put it in the only storage facility she had. The handsome plant was subsequently named *E. amygdaloides* var. *robbiae*. It wanders around in deep shade, displaying shiny dark-green rosettes and producing acid-yellow croziers by April, but it is never invasive and is easily restricted. The beauty of Mrs Robb is that she performs in the blackest corner of the garden – although she will inevitably stray away from it. Native bluebells (*Hyacinthoides non-scripta*) peak at exactly the right moment to create a sparkle with her.

The common wood spurge (*E. amygdaloides*), widespread in Europe and North Africa and often found in deep shade in woodland, is not a rambler. It produces an evergreen clump of foliage, but the flowers are lime-green rather than bright acid-yellow. There are purple-leafed forms, and the combination of

Milium effusum 'Aureum'
with *Ranunculus ficaria*
'Brazen Hussy'; *Euphorbia*
× *martini*.

beetroot-purple leaves and lime-green on a plant that usually
reaches up to 60 centimetres (2 ft) feet in height at most is
very attractive. Use the dark, sultry foliage as a foil for such
pallid narcissi as N. 'W.P. Milner'. The finest form of the
native spurge is 'Craigieburn', which has the largest and
most substantial rosettes of foliage.

Other hybrids of E. *amygdaloides* include the diminutive
'Blackbird', a dark-leafed form with small lime-green heads.
This is a good container plant, but in a border it would have
to grace the front. E. 'Whistleberry Garnet' is more allied to
Mrs Robb, with large rosettes of sumptuous foliage in velvet-
green. As winter descends, the undersides and margins of
the leaves develop a warm blush that flatters the lime-green
flowers to perfection. However, its winter presence is even
more valuable because the foliage seems to shine in the bleak
midwinter. I also rate another spurge with chartreuse-green
flowers, E. × *martini*, a hybrid of wood spurge and the silver sun-
loving Mediterranean species E. *characias*. The foliage of E. ×
martini is a soft grey-green and the flower heads are carried
up to 60 centimetres (2 ft) high. Each flower is studded with a
warm tomato-red eye, so this poised plant has real eye appeal.

The lime-green theme can be continued with one of the
best winter-flowering evergreens for deep shade, another

native: *Daphne laureola*, the spurge laurel. Few plants possess such leathery dark foliage, arranged in neat rosettes like motifs on an old-fashioned bathing cap. This low, round evergreen (which can attain 1.5 metres/5 ft in height in time) is graced by honey-scented lime-green flowers, which emerge half-hidden among the top leaves. A rarer form, *D. laureola* subsp. *philippi*, has fluted, ragged-edged, yellow-green flowers. This plant is found growing naturally in the Pyrenees, and it's shorter and more prostrate than the ordinary form – reaching barely 60 centimetres (2 ft) – but I prefer the simplicity of ordinary *D. laureola*. If your garden is large, the red-edged green flowers of another native, the unattractively named stinking hellebore (*Helleborus foetidus*), make a good companion.

Those with even more room could use the plain lime-green flowers and jagged shiny foliage of the Corsican hellebore, *H. argutifolius*. Within a year or two it will arrange itself into the spokes of a wagon wheel and lie prone on the ground – hence the need for extra room. Apple-green hybrid hellebores are easier to accommodate in smaller spaces.

Once late April comes, another fiery euphorbia emerges, tall and airy with dusky orange colouring: *E. griffithii*. The two common forms are 'Dixter' and 'Fireglow'; 'Dixter' is shorter so there is sense in planting both. Both these spring torches start with spears of fiery apricot-orange piercing the earth, before sultry burnt-orange inflorescences uncurl above darkly ribbed foliage. These Himalayans run about in cool soil, popping up here and there, and can make a real impact, even in shade, teamed with such sultry tulips as 'Havran' and 'Prinses Irene'. Or add the best allium of all for May:

A. *hollandicum* 'Purple Sensation'. Its green foliage, which always looks battered by April, needs to emerge through or behind something, but the purple orb is a very pleasing colour, without a hint of the silver-grey shared by later-flowering sun-lovers.

Later in the year, taller, more substantial acid-yellow euphorbias join the show, including the much taller E. *palustris*, a lover of good soil. Given good conditions, this summer dazzler will reach 1.5 metres (nearly 5 ft). However, the stems tend to flop, so this is one plant that will need staking, and a hazel frame is the best way. Most euphorbias can happily stay upright on their own.

E. *wallichii*, a self-supporting euphorbia with emerald-green leaves midribbed in white, also makes a valuable garden plant, for good soil in a cooler spot in the garden. Cultivars vary in ease of growing, height and flowering time, ranging from 60 centimetres/2 ft to a willowy 90 centimetres/3 ft, and from late May to July. One of this euphorbia's charms is the triangular arrangement of the top yellow cyathium leaves: it looks rather like a spear.

Opposite: Bluebells (*Hyacinthoides* sp.), *Tulipa* 'Queen of Night' and alexanders (*Smyrnium olusatrum*).

Above: *Euphorbia griffithii* 'Fireglow'.

Below: *Allium hollandicum* 'Purple Sensation'.

Spring Green

The garden will never be quite as lush and fresh again, and the foliage seems to make more of an impact on the eye than the flowers.

Lush green foliage, newly emerged after its winter sleep, frames virginal white flowers to perfection, creating elegance and harmony.

White and green is an elegant scheme, but also a soothing one, and the easiest time of year for most gardeners to achieve this simple blend is in late spring, when foliage is fresh and verdant and the light is still soft. In bright light, pure white burns out and looks harsh and icy, so if you aspire to a white-and-green garden in summer you have to cast some shade. Strong sunshine also sends white flowers over quickly, because their petals contain much less pigment than those of coloured blooms. As a result the cells contain more air gaps, so in strong light the flowers brown and die badly. It all means that once summer comes, good white flowers are best in semi-shade. Grand gardens (such as Sissinghurst) often have mature yew hedging, which acts as a rich green backdrop and casts a shadow in which the whites glow warmly. Fortunately, many white flowers have good green foliage, and that isn't just the effect of the two colours together. It is noticeable even before the flowers appear in *Geranium macrorrhizum* 'White-Ness', for instance, that the foliage is a much softer green than that of other geraniums.

Below: *Dryopteris erythrosora*; *D. filix-mas*.

Opposite: The upright fronds of the shuttlecock fern (*Matteuccia struthiopteris*) emerge to frame the pink Tiffany lamps of *Erythronium revolutum*. This scheme demands moisture-retentive soil.

Although a white-and-green border will peak in early May in a quiet, shady corner of the garden – possibly against a hedge or close to yew or box – white is one of the first colours to make an impact in the garden, when the snowdrops push through the earth (see pp. 143–44). By May, the foliage of all early bulbs is withering horribly, so if you include snowdrops in this border you will need to camouflage the dying brown leaves by using a plant that will produce a soft sheath of foliage by April. The very best plant for this effect is the fern, and one genus obligingly unfurls its fronds in early May: *Dryopteris*.

Although *Dryopteris* translates from the Greek as 'oak fern', the first three letters should be used as an aide-memoire to remind you that many of these handsome ferns can cope with drier conditions in shade. However, dry shade is considered to be the worst gardening position of all, and any plant that is introduced into this hostile environment must be carefully nurtured during its first season. Planting small specimens also helps. Use a specialist fern nursery (Fibrex is the only one to specialize in hardy ferns) to find the finest on offer, because ferns offer great variety and texture and should be a keynote in any white-and-green late-spring border in shade or semi-shade.

Ferns are primitive non-flowering plants and throw up lots of variation because of their simple genetic structure, which provides them with only one copy of each chromosome. More highly developed plants are diploid: they have two of each, and the second backs up the first should

that fail. If a chromosome fails or is missing in a fern, however, there is no backup, so effectively a random system operates, throwing up variations over time. The words *cristata* (crested), *crispa* (crinkled/curled), *grandiceps* (large points) and *congesta* (very close together) crop up often in the Latin names of ferns.

Most British ferns were collected from the wild by sharp-eyed Victorians during the fern-crazy era of pteridomania, which seems to have begun in 1830 and peaked in 1870. It is said that bonneted Victorian ladies, armed with wicker baskets, entirely denuded the area around London in their enthusiasm. Native ferns are prevalent in the wetter western and northern half of Britain, and these wilder areas became accessible to ordinary people for the first time when the railway system began to operate. The introduction in 1829 of the Wardian case, a covered glass box originally used to transport newly discovered plants by ship, made it practical to keep ferns even if you didn't have the means to build a Victorian fernery, and if you did, Pulhamite (an artificial stone) was the ultimate essential when re-creating the natural habitat.

As gardeners, we are still reaping the benefits of this pillaging, and many ferns bear the name of the person who discovered the form. Martindale (*Dryopteris filix-mas* 'Cristata Martindale', discovered in the Lake District in 1872), Wills (*D. filix-mas* 'Grandiceps Wills', Dorset, 1870), Mrs Frizzle (*Athyrium filix-femina* 'Frizelliae', County Wicklow, Ireland, 1857) and Wollaston (*Polystichum setiferum* 'Divisilobum Wollaston', Devon, 1852) are just four that are still with us. Ferns that

disappeared through being over-collected have often recolonized their favourite haunts, because ferns have a juvenile 'liverwort' stage that escaped collection.

New fern fronds are glorious affairs, with an aura like that of newborn babies. *Dryopteris* are the most handsome and upright of all wintergreen ferns, outshining all others in spring. (Wintergreen plants, as the name implies, produce foliage during the winter – although they may get weatherbeaten – and die back in summer.) Most of these ferns unfurl their coiled croziers at the end of April, coinciding with native bluebells in the wild. In the garden this foliage is normally cut right down in December, when it gets shabby, to reveal bumpy brown knuckles. (Snowdrops can be tucked tightly into and around these knuckles. As they open they shine next to the hairy brown of the ferns, and as the new fronds expand they cover the withering snowdrop foliage at just the right moment.) As well as *Dryopteris*, there are other wintergreen ferns that are easy to grow, and with so much variation it is hard to make generalizations, but I shall attempt it.

Polypodies (literally 'many-footed', because they have creeping rhizomes) have good winter foliage and leathery leaves with a slight sheen that seems to allow them to shrug off cold weather. However, *Polypodium cambricum* (the southern polypody) dies back in spring before putting out new fronds in late summer or autumn. All polypodies are dormant in summer, which is the time to divide and propagate them. Spring is a good time to tidy them, however. Polypodies need better drainage than many ferns, and they prefer an airy position on limy soil, often placing themselves on a slope or wall in the wild. The fronds bend towards the ground and the general outline tends to be a wide hummock.

Polystichums (the name meaning 'many rows') are works of art: some are intricate mossy affairs that catch raindrops on their relaxed, gently arching fronds; others are almost feathery enough to look like a section cut from an old-fashioned paper doily. All are forms of the soft-shield fern (*P. setiferum*), a light-green tactile fern, often with intricately lacy fronds. Those of the Divisilobum Group are the mossiest of all, and 'Plumoso-divisilobum Esplan' is probably the loveliest of the mossy ones. 'Herrenhausen' has always been a favourite of mine because of the way the tips of the fronds curl up, cocooned in white silk. This is an intricate doily. Others are more feathery in form; 'Pulcherrimum Bevis' bears more upright fronds in darker green, each tapered to a very fine point. This is a fern for minimalists, with delicate leaflets suspended on the narrowest brown midrib. All polystichums prefer good drainage, and all unfurl their S-shaped croziers in spring.

Polystichum setiferum 'Pulcherrimum Bevis'.

Polystichum setiferum Plumosum Group.

Dryopteris wallichiana;
D. filix-mas.

They can look ragged in hard winters, though, so I generally tidy them in early spring unless the weather is still severe.

The most handsome of all dryopteris is Wallich's fern (D. *wallichiana*). Forms vary, but you must aspire to grow the Himalayan form with black bristles that flatter the neat green fronds. There are boring rusty-brown bristled versions, so this is one plant you shouldn't order from a website: buy on sight, not reputation. I also feel that the Himalayan form is far hardier than many others because this fern has a huge range. It is found in Mexico as well as Japan, China and most of the rest of Asia. In North America (where I suspect mainly Mexican forms are grown) it has a reputation for dying in cold winters.

The other useful dryopteris is the tall, upright male fern (D. *filix-mas*) in all its forms, from 'Crispa Cristata' with its crested tips and top to 'Cristata Martindale' with its tasselled ends. Both are robust with dark-green leaves, and adore shade. For a lighter position, use the very similar D. *affinis* (the golden shield fern) for its slender, very upright habit and gingery presence. D. *affinis* subsp. *cambrensis* 'Crispa Barnes' has the fullest fronds, but I love the cockaded top of D. *affinis* 'Polydactyla Mapplebeck' and the fuller curves of 'Grandiceps Askew'.

White Highlights for Spring

Once you've established a green backbone (see pp. 133–39),
it's time to add the clean-white highlights. White tulips are
essential, and years of experimentation (and disappointment)
have taught me the value of the viridiflora tulip 'Spring
Green'. This is a vision of white and green and not too tall,
so it's a very poised affair. The green streaking on the petals
(shared by all viridifloras, hence their name) seems to make
the flowers tougher and more resilient, so they last much
longer than many. Although I am not a fan of other viridifloras
with pink, orange and green, or yellow varieties, this cool
combination of white and green is a necessity. 'Spring Green'
has another advantage: it is one of the most perennial tulips
of all, and will return for many years, although the flowers
become smaller over time. I'm fond of this downsizing. 'White
Triumphator', a tall, elegant lily-flowered tulip for early May,
and 'Swan Wings', a fringed late-flowering tulip, are also
excellent. White muscari (principally M. *botryoides* 'Album') can
add a snowflake presence, but at less than 15 centimetres
(6 in.) in height they need to be placed in view.

Another green-and-white combination is the slender
catchfly, *Silene fimbriata*. Tucked away in deepest shade, this

slightly wandering plant will pop up and deliver an airy wand of white campion flowers, each one contained in an inflated lime-green balloon of a calyx. This obliging silene does not self-seed or invade, and it retreats underground every winter to return anew. It could be allowed to mingle with white aquilegias, one very consistent strain of which, with wide-winged flowers tipped in green, used to be known as 'Munstead White' until well-meaning botanists relegated it to *Aquilegia vulgaris* 'Nivea'. Now this stable plant is mixed up with ordinary white granny's bonnets, although Long Acre Plants in Somerset have the correct form.

Aquilegias need managing in a garden, and that means removing most of the spent flowers in order to prevent thousands of seedlings. Seed heads should not be added to a compost heap, either; get rid of them elsewhere. If you want to grow aquilegias, beg, borrow or steal some pods – they are much more likely to grow well than packeted seeds sown in spring.

Although aquilegias are highly promiscuous and the gardener never knows what will arrive, certain strains are stable. Seeds collected from them produce replicas of their parents, and the pink-and-green-quilled *A. vulgaris* var. *stellata* 'Nora Barlow' is a good example. This plant was described by John Gerard in 1597 and John Parkinson in 1629, long before Alan Bloom in the 1960s named it after Charles Darwin's granddaughter. The subtle flowers could be added as a fleck of colour to pure-white borders, although several must stand together to make any impact, as Nora is willowy. 'Magpie'

Aquilegia vulgaris var. *stellata* 'Nora Barlow'; *A. vulgaris* 'William Guiness'.

(syn. *A. vulgaris* 'William Guiness') is another stable strain, and this pied white and dark-purple single aquilegia really does emulate the iridescent foliage of a magpie. The white border needn't be too purist, so both could be added.

White honesty could also be used, and there are variegated and green-leaved forms of *Lunaria annua*. Despite the species name *annua*, this plant is biennial, so you may well get a 'one year on, one year off' scheme. It will produce ragged papery pennies if left to self-seed. I have opted for two perennial forms: one is the lilac-white, scented *L. rediviva*, a large clump-former that produces diamond-shaped seed heads that stay green for months; the other is *L. annua* 'Corfu Blue', an April-flowering perennial honesty (despite its name) with the same depth of purple-washed blue found in summer-flowering phloxes. Grow it in shade, where it will shine.

The double form of the fair maids of France (*Ranunculus aconitifolius* 'Flore Pleno') is a member of the buttercup family, Ranunculaceae, named after *Rana*, the frog. That reminds us that most members of this family (including aconitums, hellebores, clematis, celandines, trollius and delphiniums) prefer a cool root run in moist but not waterlogged soil – rather like the frog. Grown since the sixteenth century, 'Flore Pleno' is thought to have come to Britain from France with the Huguenots, and this double white buttercup is the most pristine plant I grow, with its crimped and frilled buttons on branching stems set above dark, divided foliage. The hint of lemon at the heart of each

Ranunculus aconitifolius 'Flore Pleno'; *Geranium phaeum* 'Album'.

flower softens any starkness, and in fertile soil it is a delight – the epitome of daintiness.

Many of the hardy white woodland geraniums also oblige with white flowers set above green leaves. *Geranium macrorrhizum* 'White-Ness' is a neat plant – quite unlike most of the sprawling macrorrhizum geraniums that flower at this time – and produces a tight cluster of backwards-curving flowers. The yellow style and long eyelash-like stamens add to the windswept look. This albino (which has green buds, too) was found in Greece in 1990 by Paul Matthews of Ness Botanic Gardens on the Wirral.

Other clean-white geraniums with a fresh, spring-like look include *G. maculatum* f. *albiflorum*, another albino, which combines large green-veined white saucers and pale-green leaves. The fingered foliage, which has five to seven points, is handsome and continues to be a feature once the flowers fade in May and June. The more wand-like, white-flowered form of *G. phaeum* (labelled 'Album') is also pleasing, although all phaeums are too free with their seeds. Their advantage is the ability to flower early, in May, even in deep, dry shade. Later in the year, the darkly divided leaves of the low, sprawling cushion-former *G. sanguineum* 'Album' could also be used in a hot, sunny spot. This is a sparkling geranium and the only true-white *sanguineum* in a sea of magenta and pink.

Another classic performer, given some moisture, is the white form of the winged viola (*V. cornuta* 'Alba'), with its widely spaced petals and rich green foliage. It will flower

profusely in April and May, and has a charming way of craning its neck around box balls or up through tulips as it stretches for the light. Many of the named forms of V. *cornuta* are soft blues or deep purple-blue, but the white form is often stronger and more perennial, and certainly purer in form. These butterfly-flowered, truly perennial pansies are remontant and so, if cut down hard straight after flowering, will bloom again. All of them must be sheared back hard in early September in order to form a tight mound that overwinters, since leggy plants often succumb to winter wetness. Generally I do not allow them to self-seed, as I want a supply of flowers throughout the growing season and must therefore deadhead.

Lamium orvala 'Album' is a superb addition in semi-shade, but it is difficult to place, owing to its raw-boned scale with thick stems, large leaves and substantial hooded white flowers. It looks as though it has been fed on steroids. I wouldn't entertain the drabber, more readily available dusky-pink version, though. Easier to place for scale are white pulmonarias, but so far a good one has eluded me. 'Sissinghurst White' has sulked and then died regularly; perhaps because of its less-than-hardy *saccharata* blood, which also sees off the lovely pale-pink 'Dora Bielefeld' (although argument rages about her affinity to any species). Instead I have used the strongly resilient 'Opal' (syn. 'Ocupol'), despite the fact that the flowers have a hint of pink at first before turning a glacial silver-blue. This plant persists and performs brilliantly. All pulmonarias abound in bee-pleasing nectar just when the bees need it the most; deadhead constantly to prevent unwanted seedlings, and tidy the leaves well in April.

Viola cornuta 'Alba'.

Podophyllum peltatum.

Spring Sorbet

*Pinks abound in late spring. Spangle them through
sultry purples and moody almost-blacks, or set off
branches of blossom against an eggshell-blue sky.*

The softness of spring, of suddenly feeling warm sun on your
back after months of cold weather, always seems to coincide
with the sight of blossom against a pastel-blue sky. I prefer the
gentler blossom of single or semi-double flowers that are not too
fully skirted, rather than those heavy-headed Japanese cherries
that menace you on city streets. In any case, many of the
renowned Japanese cherries make huge trees and they tend
to shine for a mere three weeks every year. As if that were not
enough, their roots undermine drains and buildings, so planting
a more modestly sized member of this family makes sense.

A good tree should offer more than three weeks of glory
and be smaller, slower-growing and longer-lived than these
giant cherries. The crab apples accommodate brilliantly, giving
both flower and fruit, and many have vibrant blooms in the
pink–purple part of the spectrum. The one I love the most is
Malus × *purpurea* 'Eleyi'; it is hard to find in Britain but seen
commonly in Dutch gardens. This small tree reaches 8 metres
(26 ft) at most and delivers its strongly pink blossom just as

Above: *Malus × purpurea* 'Eleyi'.

Below: *Tulipa* 'Jan Reus'; T. 'Recreado'.

the purple leaves unfurl, so it makes an impact. The flowers are prominent and do not get swamped by the purple foliage. Rounded red fruits follow in late summer and (as with many crab apples) tend to hang on through winter.

Unfortunately many purple-leafed crab apples are prone to disease, so perhaps it's better to grow the healthier hybrid M. 'Harry Baker', which is also easier to source. It produces the same purple-pink blossom and dark leaves, but its ruby-red crab apples are larger than average. You could use any pink-tinted blossom (stark white summons up the bleak, wintry blackthorn to country types like me), but the darker purple-pink blossom blends with late April and May tulips in shades of pink, purple and dark maroon.

Combining several colours of tulip on the purple-pink theme offers the gardener many advantages. Heights differ, giving a more natural effect and reducing the tablecloth look familiar from municipal displays. Flowering times can be extended from April until May, giving you four to six weeks of colour, by using a mixture of early and late cultivars.

You must include the Triumph tulips, which are grown en masse for the cut-flower market and produce their egg-shaped blooms during the second half of April. Triumphs – appropriately named, since more breeding has gone into this group than any other – come in the widest range of colours, with thick petals, and at about 50 centimetres (no more than 2 ft) in height they weather the spring storms well.

The bicoloured ones are often better on their own, with the exception of 'Couleur Cardinal', a scarlet shaded in plum. Plain tulips mix best, but when combining varieties you should always aspire to plant in fifties (at least) and preferably in hundreds. It's cheaper to buy in bulk, and it will never look like multicoloured sparkles on a trifle.

When it comes to pinks and purples the following Triumph varieties are all superb and will blend. The fuchsia-pink 'Barcelona' has a magenta edge that dazzles among darker shades. 'Don Quichotte' is a vibrant pink, while 'Havran' is a dusky maroon, sometimes twin-headed and not everyone's favourite. The colour of 'Jan Reus' is technically 'chrysanthemum crimson', but it's the darkest of all, with brown-red overtones. 'Rems Favourite' is a feathered purple; 'Shirley' develops a purple marbling from creamy white petals (leading to a panic that you've planted the wrong thing); and 'Negrita' is a veined beetroot-purple. These are all superb tulips that are easily available, but if you can grow only one, choose 'Negrita'.

Tulipa 'Shirley'; *T.* 'Negrita'.

The joy of Triumph tulips is that their flowers are a manageable size: not too oval and enormous. They can underpin later, taller tulips on long stems, and these could include the most popular dark tulip of all, 'Queen of Night', which is always described as a deep velvety maroon. There is a double version, 'Black Hero', which eventually turns into an almost black artichoke of a flower; since its discovery I have always had to plant it. 'Recreado' is a doge purple, while 'Bleu Aimable', a lilac-blue cockade, is always the latest tulip of all, hanging on until the second half of May. Vary the shapes by adding a lily-flowered or fringed tulip for flowers in late April to early May. Among the best for this pink-purple scheme are the lily-flowered 'China Pink', the darker 'Burgundy', and 'Jacqueline', a deep rosy pink. The fringed 'Curly Sue' is a glowing purple, but avoid the peach-pink 'Bell Song', which – as with all orange-based pinks – is desperately hard to place.

Planting tulips is quite simple. Scatter each variety separately to get an even and natural-looking mixture, making sure that the gaps between bulbs are roughly the same. They need to be planted to a depth of 10–15 centimetres (4–6 in.) if your ground allows. The most important thing is to plant in colder weather, once you feel a nip in the air – usually in November in the northern hemisphere. Planting at that time discourages a fungal disease called tulip fire (*Botrytis tulipae*), which can spot the leaves and petals with grey-green lesions. It is more likely to thrive in the warmer, moister conditions of early autumn. If you do see signs of the fungus, remove and destroy the bulbs straight away, but don't add them to your compost heap as this may harbour problems for the future. You can discourage the disease by removing tulips after flowering and then planting those for next year in a different place. Avoid buying or planting any bulbs that show blue mould, as they may have the fungus already. Planting can take place right up to Christmas without problems, as long as the soil is frost free so that you are able to dig. All commercial bulbs are treated with fungicide, so always wash your hands after handling them.

If possible I try to leave my tulips in the ground and allow them to come back, while adding freshly planted ones. Many do flower for four or five years, and they produce blooms that get smaller year after year – something I like – although you

mustn't try this if you have a problem with blight. These differences in scale help to dilute the 'big-egg' size of newly planted tulips, adding a natural touch. If you ever manage to visit Mainau, a garden beside Lake Constance in Germany, this effect is very obvious on the grassy banks, where tulips have been naturalized for decades.

Blossom doesn't always have to shine against the sky. The shrubbier cherry *Prunus incisa* 'Kojo-no-mai' is a vision of blush-pink blossom every March. This is the twiggy cherry that crowds garden centres every Easter, its meandering bare branches hardly visible between the flowers. I resisted buying it for years, convinced that it had been encouraged to produce this ridiculous amount of flower in a hothouse. Finally I succumbed and was astounded when it budded up heavily, as it has done every single year since.

If I had done my research, I wouldn't have been surprised. *P. incisa* or the Fuji cherry, as it is commonly called, is found growing wild on the volcanic slopes of Mount Fuji, which is often shrouded in low cloud. In fact, in seven trips to Japan during June (when the rainy season strikes) I have seen the mountain only once – very fleetingly from a coach window. The dwarf form of this cherry, 'Kojo-no-mai', is popular in Japan, where it is often used for bonsai. It was also admired by

the great cherry expert and hybridizer Collingwood 'Cherry' Ingram, who rated it fifth in his personal top ten (*A Garden of Memories*, 1970).

Prunus incisa is the parent of many splendid yet subtle hybrid cherries, including the white *P.* 'Umineko', the shell-pink 'Okamé' and the winter-flowering *P.* × *subhirtella* 'Autumnalis'. *P. incisa* 'Praecox', a larger shrub or small tree, is winter-flowering, and another named early form, *P. incisa* 'February Pink', has pale-pink flowers in winter and early spring, followed by tiny reddish, rounded fruits. A new form, 'Mikinori', named after the Japanese botanist and plant collector Mikinori Ogisu, has semi-double pale-pink flowers with crimson eyes, their petals frillier than those of 'Kojo-no-mai'. All forms produce beautiful autumn colour, and the serrated leaves usually turn from mid-green to yellow, with some forms developing red or purple hues.

Several spring-flowering clematis from the rather uninspiringly named Atragene Group, a mixture of alpina, macropetala, koreana and chiisanensis species, could be used in your spring sorbet of pinks and purples. However, this group of

Clockwise from top left:
Clematis macropetala;
C. 'Frances Rivis';
C. 'Markham's Pink';
C. 'Constance'.

four all need excellent drainage to do well. They also look dead in winter, and this stage must be endured since they cannot be cut back hard, although you may tidy them gently after flowering. In spring they come back to life, plumping up their buds, forming new spring-green foliage as they flower. Their constitution and natural provenance make most suitable for windy, cool corners, so they can survive where others die.

To generalize, the alpinas have neat, single flowers consisting of four petals; the macropetalas have wispy skirts with lots of petals; the koreanas have simply shaped flowers with thickly textured petals; and the chiisanensis clematis have nodding yellow flowers. In reality they have joined forces and hybridized. Many of them are blue, and a good form of the ragged-skirted, powder-blue *C. macropetala* cannot be beaten. C. 'Columbine' has an extra touch of green in the middle of the powder-blue and always looks wonderful in April. There are myriad blues – single and raggedly double.

You may wish to stick to pink, however, and *C. alpina* 'Jacqueline du Pré' has single pink flowers with a silver margin to each thick petal. C. 'Willy' is wispier, with pale-pink petals blotched in pink; 'Constance' is a strong, deep pink; and 'Ernest Markham' has a softer look. 'Tage Lundell' (raised in Sweden by the breeder of that name) has been a breakthrough colour: this obliging clematis puts out single bells of rose-purple flowers in April. The long sepals have a twisting tendency that charms the eye. This also flowers again during the year and is often out in August. (There is a viticella named 'Mrs T. Lundell', though; don't confuse the two.) 'Brunette' is a dull mahogany-red, perfect behind paler pinks.

One could do worse than emulate Vita Sackville-West's idea at Sissinghurst in Kent, of planting two alpina clematis in a tall container so that they spill and mingle from the top. This allows you to see the delicate flowers. I would be inclined to ignore the montanas, those wall-covering blue-pink clematis that peak as the apple blossom opens, because their colours tend to be cooler and harder, but they are useful if you have a barn, garage or building to camouflage. They are less hardy and should be only tidied lightly after flowering, if needed.

Classic Alternatives

This is also the season for ebony and ivory combinations of tulips mingled with later-flowering white narcissi. Classic schemes include T. 'Queen of Night' and *Narcissus* 'Cheerfulness', a piano-key combination that can be naturalized in grass. The even later single poet's narcissus (N. 'Actaea') also works well in this elegant mixture for late April and early May.

With so much opportunity to use dark, almost black tulips in your garden, you should seize the chance of adding extra drama by using orange, a colour that is often ignored. This could be a wonderfully bronzed tulip, such as 'Cairo',

Tulipa 'Abu Hassan': don't shy away from orange – it sets the garden alight.

a relatively new cultivar with a metallic patina. The long-flowering *Geum* 'Prinses Juliana' (which sends up airy wands while the tulips are in flower) is also wonderful now. This frilly geum is one of the seven plant wonders of the world, because it will flower for many weeks and its presence will add movement and light. Orange perennial wallflowers, including *Erysimum* 'Apricot Twist', or those with orange in their motley (such as 'Constant Cheer' and 'Parish's') could add extra sparkle.

Finally, if you're still at the planning stage and planting the garden framework, you may be considering a hedge as a backdrop. Experience has taught me the value of hornbeam (*Carpinus betulus*), a plant that leafs up by the middle of April, thus providing a verdant backdrop for spring-flowering plants. Beech (*Fagus sylvatica*), on the other hand, is one of the last to go green, and will look brown and dull just when your spring sorbet is at its peak. Soil is important, however, and may dictate which you plant. Hornbeam is for colder places with heavier soil, whereas beech is better on well-drained ground. A lot of gardeners, able to grow both, could make a choice.

Summer Softness

As spring glides into summer, the first fully petalled flowers unfurl as roses, peonies and lavender scent the air with a promise of things to come. A soft palette of pale colour is highlighted by deep magenta detail.

There's a softness about summer that's special to this season, and the flowers tend to reflect the gentle mood. Fragrant, full-petalled peonies and roses are followed by the short spikes of Oxford-blue English lavender supported by a host of hardy geraniums in shades of blue, white and pink. Don't choose too many baby blues and pinks, though: they will look insipid every time the sun casts its bright eye. Embroider the scheme by using the whole palette, and pull in strong orchid-pinks, magentas, murrey (a sombre, sexy purple found in old roses) and maroon. These colours flatter pastels and add all-important depth and tone amid the rich-green foliage. Gold and silver leaves should not feature here.

Peonies epitomize early summer, but you need to cultivate one group in particular for a lasting and extravagant show: the *Paeonia lactiflora* hybrids. These highly bred peonies are easily grown and long-lived: they flower from mid-May until

June and produce showy blooms mainly in white and pink. They are versatile and survive well as long as the ground is not too wet and cold for their tuberous roots in winter. These Chinese varieties are entirely different beasts from the cottage-garden peony (*P. officinalis*), which graced our ancestors' gardens. The latter is shorter in stature and flowers in early May, lasting for a week or two at the most before it fades and flops.

Peonies can also be moved. The old wives' tale that they cannot has its roots in old superstition. The ancient Greeks revered the potent peony for its medicinal uses, and even named it after the physician of the gods, Paeon. They believed that a woodpecker would peck out your eyes if you dug up the plant, and this preposterous theory stuck. Peonies do move, honestly; mine have moved three times in ten years and they have flowered well. It is best done in autumn, just as the foliage dies down. The trick is to keep the tubers only 5 or so centimetres (a couple of inches) below the soil surface. Plant them any deeper and they will refuse to flower. Peonies are greedy feeders, and they are one of a handful of plants that should be given extra food. Cut down the foliage as it starts to fade and feed them with a balanced garden fertilizer. Feed them again in spring once the foliage has begun to unfurl.

P. lactiflora varieties have been bred and selected in China for centuries. Many were bred for the cut-flower trade in the mid-nineteenth century, just when the rail system began to allow faster transit earlier in the morning. European breeding began in England, but was taken up by such important French breeders as Victor Lemoine of Nancy (1823–1911). As a result, many of the best (although not all) have alluring French names that reflect their breeding. The British firm Kelways (once the biggest nursery in the world) carried out its own breeding programme between 1880 and 1920, naming 500 varieties. In the twentieth century American breeders were the most involved, and they have widened the colour range to include red. There are singles, semi-doubles and doubles, and all have a blowsy, Rubenesque quality that painters have adored for centuries. The double flowers sometimes lack elegance, but they always last longer. This is largely true across the plant world: single flowers fade more quickly.

After a period of neglect, peonies are now riding high in the style stakes, and deservedly so. Modern designers have used them at the hugely influential Chelsea Flower Show in London principally because they bloom in May. Tom Stuart-Smith, a man who adores good green foliage, has brought them back into the public eye as much for leaf as for flower. The handsome greenery is a real feature throughout the

The feathery foliage of bronze fennel (*Foeniculum vulgare* 'Purpureum') adds extra opulence to the bowl-shaped peony 'Buckeye Belle' and deep-red astrantias in this planting by Luciano Giubbilei. But it's the deep blue, provided by *Iris* 'Superstition' and *Salvia nemorosa* 'Caradonna', that lights the touchpaper visually.

growing season, and a natural partner for the foliage of roses, with which it shares a glossy constitution and rounded leaf shape. Usefully, many peonies pre-empt and then overlap with the roses. Their flower forms are similar and their colour palette blends with old-rose colours.

The hybrid 'Buckeye Belle' is a bowl-shaped lustrous-red peony that gets its colour from the cottage-garden peony *P. officinalis*. It flowers early because of its lineage. It was awarded the American Peony Society Award for Landscape Merit in 2009, so it does well in larger planting schemes as well as in the garden. This almost single-flowered form copes

well with shade, as do many single peonies, including
P. lactiflora 'White Wings'. There is also one called P. 'Chocolate
Soldier', which is a dull brown-red that will need a rich-green
background to prevent it getting lost.

The *P. lactiflora* hybrids are handsome and taller than the
cottage-garden peonies, and a mature plant can produce forty
or fifty flowers – hence their popularity as a cut flower. Ants
will continually lick off the sticky coating from the tight buds,
but they do not harm the plant. With so many flowers, it
should go without saying that staking is a necessity, and
tall semicircular iron hoops do the job best. Rain weighs the
flowers down, but peonies are resilient creatures, used to
the heavy downpours of the Asian rainy season. Peony scent
is a heavenly feature of some hybrids.

The best peonies have strong stems, and include the
following fully petalled varieties. The fragrant *P. lactiflora*
'Festiva Maxima', a pale-pink maroon-flecked peony that
fades to white as it opens, is the one to use among sultry
roses because the pale, milky flowers stand out well. The
maroon fleck picks up dark rose shades, and you can enhance
the effect by adding heavily spotted white and pink foxgloves
(just the ordinary *Digitalis purpurea*). These biennials form the
rosette of leaves one year and the flowers the next, so it's vital
to put in new plants annually to avoid the 'one year on, one
year off' problem from which all biennials suffer.

P. lactiflora 'Edulis Superba' is a deep magenta with an
ostrich-feather texture, and could flatter a creamy rose, such
as the modern, award-winning Kordes floribunda 'Champagne
Moments' ('Korvanaber'). *P. lactiflora* 'Solange' is a vision of

palest pink and white, held on dark stems. 'Félix Crousse' is a magenta-purple that was so good the breeder decided to name it after himself. But if there's room for just one, plant 'Duchesse de Nemours', a lemon-scented creamy white.

There are too many good roses to home in on here, but the ones I grow have to be healthy, not too tall (a little over 1 metre/3 ft at most) and repeat-flowering. Kordes roses, bred in Germany without the support of black-spot sprays, etc., are high on my list as they are selected for resistance to disease. 'Joie de Vivre' ('Korfloci 01') is a recent free-flowering healthy rose with blush-white blooms aplenty. 'Rhapsody in Blue' ('Frantasia') is a single floribunda rose with clusters of violet-blue flowers – one of the few in this sultry colour. When combined with the mid-blue hardy *Geranium* 'Orion' it radiates a smoky heat, making the blue saucers of 'Orion' more dramatic. R. 'Pearl Drift' ('Leggab') is another personal favourite, with its silver-pink buds that open into silver-white single blooms; its mid-green shiny foliage is almost as good as its flowers.

There are lots of plants that will act as a starter to this scheme, including violas and tulips in soft pale pinks and mauves, before the peonies start to lead on the roses. London Pride (*Saxifraga × urbium*) shares the peonies' glossy foliage, producing rosettes topped by 30-centimetre (1-ft) wands of frothy white-and-pink sprays. Good forms include 'Miss Chambers' and the related S. × *geum* Dixter form. *Heucheras* and their close relatives × *Heucherella* are also useful, especially × *Heucherella* 'Kimono', with its jade-green fingered leaves zoned in maroon. 'Tapestry', a veined mix of purple and

Above: *Heuchera* 'Silver Scrolls'.

Below: *Rosa* 'Rhapsody in Blue' ('Frantasia'); R. 'Pearl Drift' ('Leggab').

Opposite: This mixture of old-fashioned *gallica* roses is set off by a pale-pink English lavender (*L. angustifolia* 'Loddon Pink') and the purple-blue *L. angustifolia* 'Hidcote'.

Above, clockwise from top left: *Lavandula angustifolia* 'Mellisa Lilac'; *L.* 'Regal Splendour'; *L. angustifolia* 'Miss Katherine'; *L. angustifolia* 'Hidcote'.

silver, is another heucherella of great charm, and *Heuchera* 'Silver Scrolls' shares its palette. These all thrive in harsh weather, their handsome leaves looking like snowflakes against the bare brown earth of winter.

Once the peonies have produced their one and only show, the roses will also have a breather as they garner their strength for a later display, normally in August. Some flowers are needed to fill the gap, and campanulas and lavenders are useful here. Both can be chopped back in mid-May to retard the flowers, so that they follow rather than coincide with the roses.

Of the lavenders, the hardy, long-lived English lavender (*Lavandula angustifolia*) responds to this 'Chelsea chop' (so called because the timing of the famous garden show reminds gardeners to do it). It flowers naturally in midsummer, producing 2.5-centimetre (1-in.) flower spikes that resemble small bottlebrushes in profile. They do not have tufted petals (as do those bred from less hardy Spanish and French species, L. *stoechas*), and they do not produce long, tapering flowers in the manner of the later-flowering but not as hardy lavendin hybrids (cultivars of L. × *intermedia*, such as L. × *intermedia* 'Grosso', 'Pale Pretender', Dutch Group and 'Old English'). Both *stoechas* and × *intermedia* species resent hard pruning, and they are merely shaped instead. The lavendins are rounded into orbs in September. If severe cutting is needed, do it in spring, taking half the bush back at a time and leaving the other half for cutting back the following year. Lavendins produce a billowing lot of stems, more sea urchin than lavender, and they make excellent specimen plants at the front of a sunny border.

The tufted lavenders, often called French or Spanish lavender (bred from L. *stoechas* and its subspecies), are the showiest of all, with fat flowers topped with flag-like tufts of varying lengths. They produce a first flush of flowers in May, and after that it is time to trim back their upright, woody frames by a third. In autumn all spent flowers should be removed, as they tend to absorb moisture and rot off once the weather turns cold and wet. 'Regal Splendour' is a fine purple form.

English lavender is hardy enough to be cut back hard in late summer – right down to the ground if necessary. This encourages the plant to produce a tight mound of growth that will overwinter well. Leggy lavenders tend not to survive. If you cut into the bushes again in early May, and remove half the new growth, the flowers will arrive in July and August, filling the rose famine. This is the technique used among the old-fashioned roses at the National Trust's Mottisfont Abbey in Hampshire. L. *angustifolia* 'Hidcote' (a pristine dark purple), 'Imperial Gem' (a less compact purple), the soft lavender-mauve 'Mellisa Lilac' and 'Twickel Purple' (a slender-flowered aromatic variety) are all excellent in sun close to roses.

Some campanulas can also be coerced into flowering later by being given a Chelsea chop in the latter half of May. However, they are a diverse lot, and the ones that are needed in this type of border are well-behaved herbaceous varieties that don't stray off and conquer next door's garden, or spread with voracity. That rules a lot out. Among those I have come to regret are the rambling *Campanula glomerata* – such a well-behaved native when starved on cliff-tops – and the aggressive 'Pink Octopus', which was far too free with its tentacles. Many *takesimana* and *punctata* varieties are

dull-pink thugs. I am now watching 'Swannables', which was ominously labelled as a spreader. It has small grey-blue bells that hang their heads 30 centimetres (1 ft) above the ground, although one wonders what's happening underneath.

The best campanula for a rose-inspired border is undoubtedly *C. lactiflora* 'Prichard's Variety' (thought to date from the 1920s). Robust enough to push up through and between roses (even shrub roses), it stays anchored in position and will also tolerate some shade, as do many herbaceous campanulas. Whenever 'Prichard's Variety' is deadheaded, it sends out more flowers within ten days. It will reach 1 metre (3 ft) in height, but the act of chopping it back in May not only makes it peak after the roses, but also reduces the height to about 75 centimetres (2–3 ft). There is a soft lilac-pink variety, 'Loddon Anna', but I have found it less resilient.

The mid-blue mopheads of 'Prichard's Variety' are admittedly not as dark as the Cadbury's milk-chocolate-foil *C.* 'Kent Belle', but the large flowers of the latter are here today and gone tomorrow. Even the sterile 'Sarastro' (which throws out flowers regularly throughout the year) bears overlarge blooms, although it's good with golds in shade. It flowers as if its life depended on it – flush after flush – and I am always thankful to see it in October.

Geranium pratense
'Plenum Violaceum'.

Well-behaved and Floriferous Hardy Geraniums

Hardy geraniums provide a baffling choice for any gardener, but having been lucky enough to see the large trial held at RHS Wisley between 2002 and 2005 I can identify some award-winning varieties of these most amenable of garden plants. They can be manipulated in the same way as campanulas, and many (if cut back hard) flower obligingly late. Others are happy to do it all again if they are sheared off after their first flush.

The most useful geraniums to the gardener are those that don't produce copious amounts of seed and unwanted seedlings, although I would make an exception for *G. pratense* 'Mrs Kendall Clark'. This upright, white-veined, lilac-blue form of the meadow cranesbill shimmers in summer sun like no other, but it does produce seeds. There are double forms of the meadow cranesbill that don't set seed; their flowers are smaller, resembling mini rosebuds. The best for colour is the deep-violet 'Plenum Violaceum'. In hot weather these flowers fade to brown, and that can be annoying – browns should occur only in autumn!

Many of the non-seeding varieties are in fact sterile hybrids that cannot be pollinated because of a pollen incompatibility caused by two closely related parents hybridizing in a garden setting. Sterile plants produce flowers non-stop – a boon in any garden. The best true-blue hardy geraniums in this sterile category are G. 'Orion' and 'Rozanne', both of which form large plants. 'Orion' is very much in the tradition of the much-loved variety 'Johnson's Blue', and will flower by May. If sheared back in July it will bloom again in late summer or early autumn. The substantial, billowing mound of divided green foliage remains fairly compact and fresh without revealing a tonsure in the centre. The violet veining is a splendid feature of 'Orion', and I like to team this plant with the ruby-red scabious *Knautia macedonica*. They flatter each other beautifully.

The long-flowering 'Rozanne' ('Gerwat') was discovered in Donald and Rozanne Waterer's garden in Somerset in 1990. It proved hard to propagate naturally and, but for micropropagation, would never have made it into commercial life at all. It is a huge improvement on *G. wallichianum* 'Buxton's Variety' – obviously one of its parents – which produces smaller flowers on a less vigorous bush in September. 'Jolly Bee' has now been identified as the same plant as 'Rozanne' by DNA analysis. 'Rozanne' has larger, paler-blue flowers than 'Orion', and they come later in the year. It's a sprawling plant with marbled foliage, both traits inherited from 'Buxton's Variety'. The deep-blue flowers have

Clockwise from top left: *Geranium pratense* 'Mrs Kendall Clark'; G. 'Rozanne'; G. 'Mavis Simpson'; G. 'Patricia'.

a paler middle and there's a hint of warm red; the whole flower is further enhanced by a neat ring of black stamens that I find irresistible. Dark stems (such as those of *Aster divaricatus*) planted close by can pick up this black detail. Some gardeners chop 'Rozanne' back hard in May so that it's more pristine and virginal in September.

'Patricia' ('Bremapat') ranks as the third sterile larger geranium that gardeners should always grow if there is space. This black-eyed magenta geranium, created by the well-known Orkney breeder Alan Bremner, is rarely out of flower, and I leave it to weave its spell untroubled by secateurs. Its *G. psilostemon* parentage allows it to do well in shade, too. It will mingle in pink-and-blue schemes or clash wonderfully with oranges, and it catches the eye wherever it's planted. Whoever Patricia was, she must have had showstopping character.

Sunny edges need lower-growing hardy geraniums, many of which have silver-green foliage, and these may be difficult

Philadelphus 'Belle Etoile'.

Verbascum chaixii 'Album'.

to keep in wet soil. Three spring to mind: the lovely white-flowered 'Coombland White' (a *G. lambertii* × *G. traversii* cross) needs warmth, light and sharp drainage before it throws out its hundreds of small lilac-veined white flowers. The soft, tactile foliage is always pleasing, too. Propagate regularly, as this plant fades after three good years. Use it on well-drained border edges with two old classics that have never been beaten: *G.* 'Mavis Simpson' and *G.* × *riversleaianum* 'Russell Prichard'. The latter was the first to arrive, in 1915, at Maurice Prichard's Riverslea Nursery at Christchurch in Hampshire (the nursery that introduced *Campanula lactiflora* 'Prichard's Variety' and *Aconitum* 'Spark's Variety'). 'Russell Prichard' has magenta flowers with veins that are almost red. The silver-pink 'Mavis Simpson' was discovered some years later at the Royal Botanic Gardens at Kew by the lady herself. It is the most beguiling of the two (and is said to be hardier, too), and it is stunning under the silvery biennial sea holly *Eryngium giganteum* – a combination used by Sibylle Kreutzberger and the late Pam Schwerdt in their private garden at Condicote in Gloucestershire. Their superb eye for colour is legendary.

Three compact ladies could also flourish in this scheme. *Geranium* 'Dilys' (a recent Alan Bremner hybrid named after Dilys Davies of the Hardy Plant Society) has dark-centred, reddish-pink flowers from June until November. 'Joy' (*G. traversii* var. *elegans* × *G. lambertii*) is also from Alan Bremner. It is named after Joy Jones, a hardy-geranium expert and co-writer of a monograph on geraniums, and has pale-pink flowers with prominent magenta veins over marbled foliage. Good drainage is essential for 'Joy' (because of her *traversii* blood), and she may not be hardy enough for some, even when given sharp drainage. The last of the trio, 'Elke', has bright-pink flowers edged in white. All three are low-growing mat-formers.

Finally, I would always use the orchid-pink *Stachys officinalis* 'Hummelo' (syn. *S. macrantha* 'Hummelo'). This produces a sheath of upright stachys flowers, an upright accent that is very necessary in a scheme of mounds and hummocks. It was bred by Ernst Pagels, but named after Piet Oudolf's nursery in The Netherlands because he popularized this stunning erect betony. Oudolf always uses it in his naturalistic schemes to great effect, as much for the seed head as for the flower.

Campanula lactiflora
'Loddon Anna'.

Cosmos bipinnatus
Sensation Series.

Another excellent vertical for this soft planting scheme is a truly perennial verbascum with maroon-eyed white flowers, *Verbascum chaixii* 'Album'. It has exactly the same colouring as the fragrant *Philadelphus* 'Belle Etoile', one of the few shrubs capable of enhancing and coinciding with pink and purple roses. This man-high shrub suits the back of the border, and you will have to remove a third of the flowering wood every year to keep it floriferous.

This type of planting needn't be hackneyed or old-fashioned as long as you fill the gaps between the plants with an airy froth of London Pride, small violas, smoky-leaved heucheras and late-season blush-white-and-pink *Cosmos* and *Gaura lindheimeri*. These will soften the larger flowers of the peonies and roses, and the last two will keep the border flowering until November.

Summer Sparkle

A swirling mass of *Stipa tenuissima* and blue-stemmed *Eryngium planum* 'Blaukappe', with Spanish lavender, creates a silver sparkle over many months in a hot spot.

Silver foliage sparkles under high summer sun, spinning through the sunniest areas of the garden, showing off lemon, sky-blue and purple-pink.

The overhead sun of summer applies a watercolour wash that seems to fade as we approach the longest day. There's a gentle ambience that explains why June can be so soothing – and yet there's also the sparkle of lots of silver foliage. Three of the best colours on offer are acid-yellow, purple and blue, perhaps with a touch of magenta for razzmatazz. This fresh, invigorating scheme can be repeated throughout the year using dahlias, spring bulbs, bedding or later-flowering perennials.

The first half of summer should give the gardener a series of sunny days, and most of the plants that come to the fore now are hardy perennials that prefer an open position in well-drained ground. The term well-drained suggests dry, light soil, but many moisture-retentive alluvial soils also drain well. My own garden (on a bleak Cotswold summit) sits on the spring line, so we are rarely short of water underground, yet the soil drains well here, and bulbous, rhizomatous and tuberous plants (including peonies and irises) do exceptionally well despite the moist soil conditions.

Foliage is always important: it sets off the flower but must also maintain a consistent background theme. Silver-leaved plants should inhabit your sunniest hot spots, and they back up lemon, blue and purple beautifully. Green is universal, but golden foliage is best in shade, where it casts light without becoming scorched. Variegated foliage that contains gold or brash yellow is warmer than leaves splashed in cooler cream. Build your carpet before you add a pattern of highlights.

Silver foliage should be the backbone of a summery 'hot-spot' border. This colour stubbornly refuses to absorb heat from the sun's rays, so silvers are better suited to full sun than other colours. However, not all gardeners can manage to grow them to advantage. Silver plants need sharp drainage and limited rainfall in order to keep their silvery sparkle and stiff stems. If you garden on heavy, damp soil, or live in an area with high rainfall, silver leaves tend to become a dull sage-green rather than a downy white, their growth habit tends to become thuggish and stems flop. This may make *Stachys byzantina* (the woolly lamb's ear) a coarse, unattractive smotherer rather than a usefully neat edger. And, sadly, your *Eryngium planum* will never develop upright, steely blue stems and thimbles, but instead will take on a much less pleasing silver-green patina.

A glorious jumble of sun-loving silvers, including plummy verbascums, *Achillea* 'Moonshine' and *Allium cristophii*, rises above aromatic artemisia.

Silvers should never be fed, since their deep root systems pick up enough nutrients. They also tend to resent being cut down before winter, because many have a Mediterranean provenance and do their growing in mild, damp winters in their homeland. They consequently provide ragged silhouettes in winter.

Artemisias, or wormwoods, could form your grey carpet, but they are a diverse bunch. Some are quite woody, others produce bright-yellow flowers that make you reach for the secateurs involuntarily, and others travel down a border with too much enthusiasm. As a general rule, the more finely divided the leaf the more drought-tolerant the plant and the more it will resent damp soil. A pungent smell and oily foliage also indicate that this plant likes to sunbathe: after all, it has produced its own sunscreen.

If you're sure your soil is well-drained, one of the best plants for silver foliage is the curly, wispy *Artemisia alba* 'Canescens', a non-running clump-former that is lovely throughout the year, making a tangle of curls in grey-white. The lower-growing *A. schmidtiana* is softer and silkier, and was described by Mrs Desmond Underwood in her famous book *Grey and Silver Plants* (1971) as a moss-covered molehill – a phrase that has stayed with me. If your garden is warm and

Above: *Artemisia ludoviciana.*

Opposite, clockwise from top left: *Allium vineale* 'Hair'; *A. sphaerocephalon*; *A. hollandicum* 'Purple Sensation'.

sheltered, the ground-hugging chrysanthemum-leaved A. *stelleriana* is a classy addition; it tolerates damper ground, although a hard winter can see it off.

If these seem too challenging for your garden, the easier option is the larger A. 'Powis Castle', a cloud-forming mound of filigree leaves that can take up a square metre (10 sq. ft) of ground by the end of summer. Cut it back hard annually once winter has truly receded. A. *ludoviciana* is the invasive option, a runner that will need regular evicting unless ground cover is needed. A. *ludoviciana* 'Valerie Finnis' has neater rosettes of foliage and silvery flower spikes that reach roughly 1 metre (3 ft) tall. Cuttings can be taken from non-invasive artemisia in summer. Snip off 7 or 8 centimetres (3 in.) or so of new growth below a leaf node and plunge the cuttings into a pot filled with either horticultural sand or a half-and-half mixture of sand and compost. The invasive ones can be ripped from the ground and replanted, although most of mine end up on the compost heap.

A carpet of foliage is essential if you want to enjoy the best ornamental onion of all: *Allium hollandicum* 'Purple Sensation'. It produces deep-violet orbs 7–10 centimetres (3–4 in.) wide by mid-May, and these are just the right size to mingle with other things. 'Purple Sensation' is also the best follow-up act for late tulips. However, by the time the glowing flower head appears the leaves have already become ragged and faded, their tips bleached and jarring against the colours of summer, so it must be planted to pop up through something else. The flowers endure as the seed head gradually develops, and the trick is to cut the head out before the copious black seeds hit the ground. That's a good recommendation with any allium; they produce a grassy swathe of unwanted seedlings otherwise.

If silvers evade you (because of too much moisture in the ground or from the heavens) the pony-tail grass *Stipa tenuissima* can be used instead. It creates a fibre-optic effect and many can be woven through the border to create a sea of waves. The new foliage is grass-green in spring but quickly bleaches to straw and canvas, and, although looking truly handsome for only four or five years on average, it is easily raised from a packet of seeds. I favour a haircut in early spring as it maintains more vigour. S. *tenuissima* is hardy, but there is a very similar fibre-optic grass called Russian

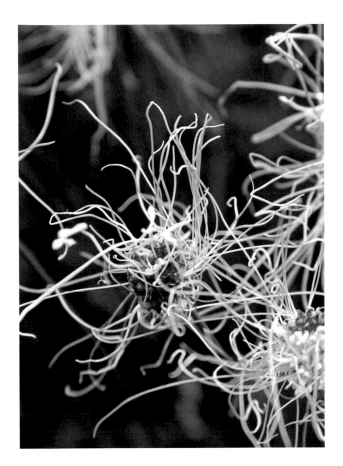

steppe grass (*S. lessingiana*), which is said to have a much tougher constitution.

Another option is the warmer-toned, much beefier *Carex testacea* (the orange New Zealand sedge), a swirling spider of foliage tinted olive-green and orange, and one of the best grasses for year-round presence. It is stunning with the fragrant terracotta tulip 'Ballerina' and the golden-eyed mauve (thankfully sterile) Jacob's ladder, *Polemonium* 'Lambrook Mauve'. A whole border could contain these three alone, they are so effective.

'Purple Sensation' is commonly available and cheap to buy, but it is still the best summer ornamental onion, thanks to its metre-high (3 ft) stiff stems and clean, colourful presence. Other tall purple alliums include A. 'Mars', 'Gladiator', *A. giganteum* and A. 'Globemaster', but they flower in June and their much larger flower heads are difficult to place well. All ornamental alliums are best planted in autumn, and the process should be repeated every three years as bulbs tend to fizzle out. Don't forget to deadhead, either. The joy of this three-year cycle is that the flowers diminish in size, and several heads in a smattering of sizes are more attractive and natural to look at.

I much prefer to plant 'Purple Sensation' with the slender drumstick allium *A. sphaerocephalon*. This small-headed

Below: *Salvia verticillata* 'Purple Rain'.

Opposite: Catmint, stachys and phlomis soften the edges of a gravel path, creating a contrast with rich evergreens.

June-and July-flowering allium has oval heads 2.5 centimetres (1 in.) wide, and a chameleon personality. It opens green and then develops maroon highlights, and it's superb with *Stipa tenuissima* and such fruity achilleas as the banana-yellow 'Credo', lemon-yellow 'Martina' and tangerine 'Walther Funcke'. The wackier, willowy *Allium vineale* 'Hair' is an Afro-styled allium with a ragged windswept look – but it is less enduring than 'Purple Sensation' or *A. sphaerocephalon*.

Two plants I can't live without at this time of year are *Anthemis* 'Susanna Mitchell' (syn. 'Blomit') and *Nepeta* 'Six Hills Giant'. This accommodating couple share silver-toned, sage-green foliage, flower at the same moment – by mid-May – and have a lax habit that allows them to hold hands and soften edges together. They can both be cut down hard in mid-July, and both can be guaranteed to flower again in September, just as prolifically. It's a marriage made in heaven. More importantly, they are consistent performers for all gardeners on all soils. Both were spotted by keen-eyed plant-lovers, having seeded serendipitously through one pollinator or another. The catmint 'Six Hills Giant' produces a perpetual flush of larger-than-average sky-blue flowers floating above small grey-green leaves. It has been with us since 1934, and was noticed by Clarence Elliott in a garden near his famous

Six Hills Nursery in Stevenage, Hertfordshire. This nurseryman's dream can be raised by pulling 'Irishman's cuttings' with a section of root away from the plant when the shoots are a few inches high. This plant will provide a billowing mound of blue for months, and it can underpin such softly hued roses as the silver-pink climber 'New Dawn' and the shrubby hybrid musk 'Penelope'. The latter has apricot-tinted flowers that fade to cream, giving the illusion of white but without icy overtones.

Anthemis 'Susanna Mitchell' arose in 1996 after being spotted by a west-country plantswoman of that name. It has feathery silver-grey foliage and hundreds of small pallid-yellow daisies held on slender stems. Less upright than other anthemis, it also flowers much earlier because of its hybrid blood, which almost certainly contains the white spring-flowering sprawler *A. punctata* subsp. *cupaniana*.

Other anthemis include some equally dazzling plants, although none repeat-flower as prolifically as 'Susanna Mitchell', a sterile hybrid. 'Sauce Hollandaise' (which could have

Sidalcea 'Sussex Beauty'
with *Anthemis tinctoria*
'Sauce Hollandaise'.

been called 'Salad Cream' by the less culinary aware) forms a tight clump and a sheath of stems bearing creamy daisies 2.5 centimetres (1 in.) wide. These don't seem to flop their ray petals downwards as larger-flowered anthemis tend to do, and the plant persists for years. A. 'Tinpenny Sparkle' has larger, pale-cream flowers and was discovered in the cold, wet, clay-bound garden – Tinpenny Farm near Tewkesbury – that was once kept by plantswoman Elaine Horton. She was out there in all weathers, in her coat and headscarf, so I suggest that 'Tinpenny Sparkle' is a toughie just like Elaine.

All larger-flowered, stiff-stemmed anthemis have short lifespans, and replacements are regularly needed, so pull pieces from the base every year and pot them up. Cutting back hard as soon as the flowers become ragged keeps the mound of growth tighter, helping to fight off winter damage. *A. tinctoria* 'E.C. Buxton' is the classic green-leaved, canary-yellow, July-flowering form. This colour is easy to use, especially with the commonly labelled *Penstemon* 'Garnet', now landed with the almost unspellable 'Andenken an Friedrich Hahn' because of its Swiss provenance. This classy plant from 1918, a lively, warm red with wine overtones, is the best and hardiest penstemon on offer, and has still not been bettered for all-round garden versatility and charm.

Anthemis tinctoria 'E.C. Buxton'; *A. tinctoria* 'Sauce Hollandaise'.

Most hybrid penstemons perform during the second half of summer, but those closely allied to shorter species are much earlier. *P. heterophyllus* 'Heavenly Blue', which shimmers between pink and blue, flowers first in May or June and then just keeps going. *P.* 'Papal Purple' is also hardly ever out of flower from June onwards. Its squat lilac-purple flowers are held on short, freely produced spikes that rarely exceed 30 centimetres (1 ft) in height. Later good cultivars from the purple spectrum include the blue-toned 'Alice Hindley', the greyer 'Sour Grapes' and the darker 'Raven' and 'Pensham Blackberry Ice'. These will reach 1 metre (3 ft) and produce upright spires.

Penstemons love sun and warmth, and actively sulk in dull summers. They are questionably hardy, so must be left intact over winter. Once they shoot from the base (usually in April), cut them back to the lowest shoots as you would a hardy fuchsia. After three years many varieties lose vigour, so do propagate by taking cuttings and plunging them into trays of damp horticultural sand.

The award for the sharpest yellow in a late-May and June performer must go to Alan Bloom's *Achillea* 'Moonshine', another plant that needs regular propagating by pulling young pieces away. Don't let that put you off, though. This acid-yellow achillea should get a gong for tenacity: a young plant

Opposite, clockwise from
top left: *Penstemon*
'Raven'; *P.* 'Pensham
Czar'; *P.* 'Sour Grapes';
P. 'Hidcote Pink'.

Right: *Salvia nemorosa*
'Ostfriesland'.

will flower from May until October, far longer and more
persistently than any other achillea. The filigree foliage is
grey, and a vigorous plant rarely succumbs in a bad winter.

Flashes of blue should be provided by a group of vibrant,
long-flowering, hardy salvias, bred mainly in Germany in the
mid-twentieth century from S. *nemorosa* and S. × *sylvestris*.
These do best in good light and warmth rather than hot, dry
heat, which tends to burn them out. They also prefer water-
retentive soil. Ernst Pagels provided the classic S. *nemorosa*
'Ostfriesland' – a striking vision of green foliage and
purple-blue spires touched with warm claret – in 1955.
The combination of red and blue always reminds me of

Salvia × sylvestris 'Dear Anja'; S. discolor.

a sooty flame flickering on a coal fire. The later S. × *sylvestris* 'Blauhügel' has distinctly lipped flowers in a softer blue. The great plantsman Karl Foerster bred 'Mainacht' in 1956, a less upright salvia with larger-lipped, deep-blue flowers held on dark stems with the merest hint of red. The recent S. *nemorosa* 'Caradonna' has airy spikes of royal-blue flowers supported by black stems. The well-named 'Amethyst' is softer, but the blue is shot through with iridescent purple, and this plant performs into autumn. I must also mention a plant I love, the double-flowered, sultry pink 'Pusztaflamme', for its presence that lasts late into the year.

These shorter hardy salvias are all fairly rocket-like and slender, and create lots of low verticals, a useful attribute in a garden flora dominated by lumpy mounds and smooth cushions. They can be woven through borders or planted in a drift at the front. They are used widely in prairie planting because, if given a severe shearing after their first flowering, they will bloom again and endure until autumn, fading into a spiky seed head.

There is another plant that curves upwards, producing a shallow bowl of blue flowers: *Salvia verticillata* 'Purple Rain'. Crinkled soft-green foliage is also a feature of this handsome, widely available plant, which was originally selected by

Beth Chatto's gravel garden provides summer sparkle followed by autumn silhouette (*Eryngium giganteum* and *Verbena bonariensis*, with agapanthus).

Piet Oudolf for its whorls of blue flowers and large midnight-purple bracts. Papery bracts feature heavily in salvias, and they play a significant role in the charm of the plant, providing contrast and extra depth of colour. The ultimate example is the black lobster that emerges from the green shell of *Salvia discolor*. The flowers of 'Purple Rain' peep out of the large bracts in a similar way. *S. verticillata* 'Smouldering Torches' (another Oudolf plant) has a more upright habit and leaves suffused with purple, but it's hard to find. Both need deadheading to prevent unwanted seedlings, which are inevitably inferior. Deadheading will also keep these plants in flower: wait until the individual branchlets begin to brown, then nip them off individually to allow more flowers to follow.

Summer Sunshine

As summer heats up, sunny oranges and yellows dominate, and here *Achillea* 'Walther Funcke' rubs shoulders with *Crocosmia* 'Lucifer', rusty heleniums and yellow anthemis.

Add some extra heat with sunshine colours that radiate warmth using a vibrant blend of oranges, reds and butter-yellow. Include a dash of sapphire-blue for extra eye appeal.

The pastel palette of early summer begins to wane as the soft sorbet of virginal pinks, pastel blues and blush-whites comes of age, and by the second half of summer, livelier, more robust colours begin to dominate, like old-fashioned debutantes doing the season. Suddenly warm yellows, fiery oranges and clear reds are available to the gardener. They can be blended to give a warm buzz, or sultry notes of blue and purple can be added to make the oranges and yellows appear more luminescent.

If you're a gardener who avoids orange on principle, take a fresh look: it can be stunning in high summer. If you decide to use it for the first time it will open up two groups of excellent garden plants – the crocosmia and the kniphofia. Both are bred from South African species and both tend to enjoy and shrug off summer rainfall. The crocosmia has sword-shaped leaves and the kniphofia produces rosettes of linear leaves (some slender and grassy, others more substantial), so they

Crocosmia 'Lucifer';
C. 'Limpopo'.

offer sculptural form as well as flowers. Both are available in a range of heights, flowering times and flower colour. In the wild many are pollinated by hummingbirds and, probably because of the strength of the South African sun, the petals are highly pigmented. So these razzle-dazzle flowers never fade in full sun.

Crocosmia 'Lucifer' announces the start of this move towards warmth and fire. By the beginning of July the bright-green pleated leaves and upward-facing rich-red flowers on this substantial plant reach 1 metre (3 ft) in height, creating a vibrancy that is rarely equalled in the plant world. And this plant is superb at every stage. The buds form a quiver of diagonals, the flowers are sumptuous and the seed head is robust. It was raised by Alan Bloom in 1969 and remains one of the most popular plants throughout the world. Most plants raised by Bloom either have the Bressingham prefix, for the Norfolk nursery he ran, or are named after family or treasured members of staff. (The latter include *Kniphofia* 'Percy's Pride', *Geranium* 'Laurence Flatman' and *Phlox paniculata* 'Eva Cullum'.) 'Lucifer' was special, however, and Bloom sensed it. It represented a huge breakthrough in breeding because most gardeners at the time grew invasive montbretias – insipid orange plants with grassy foliage. There were showier members of the tribe (which was then split between *Antholyza*, *Curtonus*, *Montbretia*, *Crocosmia* and *Tritonia*), but many were not considered to be hardy enough for garden use. The savage

Crocosmia × crocosmiiflora
'George Davison' is one of
the best yellow crocosmias
for late summer.

British winter of 1963 disproved this fallacy. All his supposedly tender crocosmias survived in the ground and this encouraged Bloom – the most single-minded plantsman I have ever met – to ask Percy Piper, his main perennial breeder, to 'dabble'. When the plant appeared, Bloom asked a Latin teacher who worked on the steam railway at Bressingham every weekend to come up with a suitably special name to reflect the plant's star quality. As the man began to ponder later that evening, he picked up a box of matches to light his cherished pipe and saw the word Lucifer on the box. The name was born.

I have found 'Lucifer' completely hardy, but I have struggled to keep others, including one I really admire: *C. × crocosmiiflora* 'Emily McKenzie'. This large-flowered, wide-eyed orange is zoned in chrysanthemum crimson, making it dusky and interesting. Although reputedly hardy, it disappears every winter for me. I have also found crocosmias with brown-tinted foliage, including 'Saracen' and 'Coleton Fishacre' (formerly 'Gerbe d'Or'), difficult to keep. Older apricot-flowered forms (often bred in France) can also succumb.

Although Bloom's 'Lucifer' was a catalyst for breeding in the latter half of the twentieth century, this group had already been widely bred in France and England, so there are a large

Dahlia 'David Howard'.

Crocosmia × crocosmiiflora 'Star of the East'.

number of named cultivars, varieties and hybrids, some dating from as far back as the 1880s. Others are much newer. My personal favourites include 'Hellfire', a tall new variety with deep-red flowers and dark stems. This all-red affair almost demands a touch of black, and the classic dahlia 'Bishop of Llandaff' could oblige. It would have the same effect as using the black strappy ophiopogon (*O. planiscapus* 'Nigrescens') with red semi-hardy cyclamen. The deep red loses any sombre quality and simply smoulders.

Crocosmia 'Carmin Brilliant' is a shining orange-red and very floriferous, reaching 1 metre (3 ft). Nothing special, but hugely reliable. My favourite burnished oranges include the species *C. masoniorum* (one of the parents of 'Lucifer') for its branching head of upward-facing flowers in brown-red. By late July or early August the flowers look like a skein of birds in full flight as they crane their necks upwards. The foliage is upright and pleated, although not as green as that of 'Lucifer'. Just like 'Lucifer', this will set seed and come true.

There are also some good sunny-yellow crocosmias. 'Paul's Best Yellow' has fully formed, large flowers that can appear between July and September. 'Walberton Yellow' and the early and vigorous *C. × crocosmiiflora* 'George Davison' are an equally good colour, but the flowers are starrier. The latter is a robust performer. All reach between 1 and 1.5 metres (3–4 ft) in height.

I have also grown three new crocosmias that have proved very hardy despite their exotic-sounding names. These sterile British-bred hybrids from the African River Series flower for much longer than most crocosmias. The best of the three, 'Limpopo', has unusually shaped pink-tinted flowers topped with a large rounded petal. The dark-leaved single dahlia 'Twyning's Revel' picks up the shot-silk colour of 'Limpopo' perfectly. (If you know 'Severn Sunrise', another excellent shimmering crocosmia for September flower, 'Limpopo' is in the same colour range.) 'Zambesi' is a warm-orange star with red shading, and the third, 'Okavango', is a warm brown-orange. All three are vigorous and tall (over 1 metre/3 ft) and they are destined to be great plants.

'Lucifer' has been dismissed by some (including the great Christopher Lloyd) because it flowers in July. I think that's a strength, however, because so many crocosmias are later. The following are among the best of the latest – often performing in October. *C. × crocosmiiflora* 'Star of the East' has enormous flat brown-orange flowers, and 'Zeal Tan' (a 60-centimetre-high/2 ft bright orange-red) is also late into flower. If your garden is warm and you have patience (it is slow to bulk up), the tallest crocosmia of all is the 2-metre-high (6 ft) *C.* 'Zeal Giant'.

Kniphofia 'Tawny King';
K. 'Painted Lady'.

Red-hot pokers, or kniphofias, offer the same breadth of choice, and the squat orange-and-yellow heads of *Kniphofia rooperi* wait until September or October to open. They emerge like pyramids – always a fascinating sight – and this is one poker I can't be without. Orange-red pokers that perform well in July include 'Fiery Fred' and 'Samuel's Sensation'. 'Fiery Fred' (which will instantly mean something to cricket aficionados) sends out lots of warm orange-red heads from June until late July, and reaches 1 metre (3 ft) in height. 'Samuel's Sensation' is much beefier, redder and later, often flowering in August and easily attaining 1.5 metres (5 ft). 'Prince Igor' is even taller, topping 2.1 metres (7 ft), with tall orange pokers that gradually produce a yellow skirt and how I wish they wouldn't. Viewed against a blue summer sky, it is one of the most handsome sights in the garden. Lots of pokers get dead tips at the top and this varies from year to year; it's caused by drought stress in the formative stages. Snails can be a great problem if they nibble the young buds, so frisk your plants well, especially early in the year.

Orange-red pokers are easier to place than those with coral overtones, and I'm less fond of 'Wol's Red Seedling' and 'Nancy's Red'. Breeders have provided us with more pokers in non-orange colours than truly blazing ones. 'Tawny King' (an

Opposite: *Kniphofia*
'Prince Igor', a beefy
orange-red poker, and
Rudbeckia laciniata
'Herbstsonne' in
my garden.

Below: *Aster × frikartii*
'Mönch'.

extremely floriferous poker with brown and apricot tints)
fits into the warm border. The cooler lime-greens can be
accommodated elsewhere, and they shine with blues and
purples. The cool-green 'Percy's Pride' (a large poker that
always has a late flush) and 'Wrexham Buttercup' are
peerless. The rich yellow of the latter opens from green buds,
and this old variety always performs well in late summer.

Most yellow daisies peak in September, but there is one
crisp rudbeckia that flowers now, and I would give it a place
in my top ten garden plants: *Rudbeckia fulgida* var. *sullivanti*
'Goldsturm'. It produces warm-yellow daisies with neat brown
middles, billowing out from a well-behaved clump (roughly up
to 1 metre/3 ft) and keeping a presence for months. This plant
has been around since 1937, and anyone can grow it. It was
spotted by Heinrich Hagemann (an employee of Karl Foerster)
in a Czechoslovakian nursery. *Rudbeckia triloba* is another
excellent brown-and-yellow daisy, producing a multitude
of small, neat blooms over months, but it is short-lived.

The natural soulmate for 'Goldsturm' is a long-flowering
soft-blue aster called A. × *frikartii* 'Mönch', a plant bred
in about 1920 by an enterprising Swiss nurseryman who
crossed the Italian aster (A. *amellus*) with a Himalayan species,
A. *thomsonii*. This inspired piece of breeding produced a

Heleniums mingle with *Agastache* 'Blue Fortune'.

drought-tolerant aster with the longest flowering season of any. The large, well-rayed flowers last for months, beginning in July. The foliage is substantial and dark green, and the stems are graceful, not woody and straight. More importantly, this aster never suffers from mildew, as do some of the highly bred North American asters developed from A. *novi-belgii*. 'Mönch' is another that would make my top ten.

It's not good planning to put two daisies next to each other, so I'd probably separate them with a sword-leaved crocosmia. More touches of blue can be provided by a branching aconitum bred in 1898: 'Spark's Variety'. It came from Maurice Prichard's nursery (see p. 64), but who Sparks was remains a mystery – one I'd love to solve. This plant is unique: the colour is a deep purple-blue, and the main stems have radiating branches that create a 45-degree angle at the stem. This arrangement provides a lot more flowers, so it clings on for months, providing a 1.2-metre-high (4 ft) branching sapphire gem in the border. Its airy silhouette breaks up stiff verticals and mounding daisies.

Aconitums are toxic at every stage, but particularly at the root, as their common name of wolfsbane warns, and some gardeners avoid them. But few plants provide strong, deep blue, and aconitums (lovers of moisture-retentive soil) can

Aconitum 'Spark's Variety'.

do it in shade because of their woodland provenance. The hooded flowers can be ivory-white, silver-grey, two-tone blue-and-white or violet-blue. The best are the rich blues, and *A. carmichaelii* 'Arendsii' (a September-flowering giant) is the best of all, with thick, downy stems clothed by hooded dark-blue flowers held above shiny dark-green foliage. This plant will extend this scheme into early autumn (see p. 113).

More summery blue glints can be added by using two agastaches with thick bottlebrushes. *Agastache* 'Blue Fortune' has a fluffy all-blue brush in a soft colour. The similar 'Black Adder' is more dramatically dark, with black undertones supporting purple-blue flowers. I have found these two hardy; not all agastaches are. Their vertical presence is particularly effective with heleniums, the best of which for most gardeners at this time of year is 'Sahin's Early Flowerer'. It was noticed in about 1995 by the late Kaas Sahin, a Dutch seedsman, in a field among thousands of similar-looking seedlings. He generously gave it to Bob Brown of Cotswold Garden Flowers in Worcestershire to bulk up, and Brown named it after his friend. This seedling flowered in June and just kept going, standing out from the throng. Each flower is slightly different, possibly because of a 'jumping gene', so the shades of yellow, rust-red and brown appear to shimmer in

sunlight. More importantly, this helenium seems to have hybrid blood that allows it to perform in drier conditions – a death sentence for most heleniums. It has deservedly taken its place in my Hall of Fame. If you've failed to grow heleniums before, please try this one. 'Luc', a newer one, is thought by some people to be even better.

Some heleniums are very short and some are too tall, and the tall ones tend to get ragged foliage at the bottom. Tucking them away behind other plants helps to hide it, but you can also do a partial Chelsea chop in May if your plant is at the front of the border. Shorten the front third of the bush to 50 centimetres (18 in.) in height, so that fresh leaves will cover any unsightly foliage. Always deadhead assiduously, because most heleniums will produce more flowers.

The most effective border heleniums average 1–1.5 metres (4–5 ft) in height. I avoid the taller ones, because they often need staking, and I dislike the pouffe-forming shorter ones, with their flowers awkwardly placed at knee-level. 'Moerheim Beauty' has a double row of mahogany-red petals that flounce downwards like an unstarched skirt, and this variety from 1930 is still considered to be the best for form and colour. There are redder ones, but this has the richness of a conker. It usually begins to flower in late July. 'Waltraut' is the classic

A touch of dark foliage, here provided by *Atriplex hortensis* var. *rubra*, sets off any orange crocosmia.

golden variety with larger flowers. The hard-to-find 'Rauchtopas' (which translates as 'smoky topaz') is the colour of warm terracotta with apricot tones over vermilion. The single row of petals curves upwards, framing the brown fuzzy centre, but unlike most heleniums this one is slow to bulk up. The time to divide any helenium is when it starts back into growth (usually in early March); use two forks back-to-back to prise the roots apart. As with any perennials that form a loose clump, the younger outer pieces are the most vigorous. Discard the middles unless you really need them.

Heliopsis are underused, but some of them provide buttons of flowers that offer a contrast to more open-rayed daisies. *H. helianthoides* var. *scabra* 'Summer Nights' is a dark-stemmed variety that branches to produce lots of single blooms that act as a foil to larger daisies. 'Asahi' produces small bright-yellow pompoms that endure for months.

Dark leaves add drama and depth in the garden, and you can use black or wine-red foliage. It has a dual role, stopping such insipid colours as apricot disappearing in full sun, and adding depth and richness to deeper colours, bringing them to life. *Cotinus coggygria* 'Royal Purple' and the black-leaved elders (*Sambucus nigra* f. *porphyrophylla* 'Eva', syn. 'Black Lace', for instance) work well. If you're growing these for foliage,

both can be cut back hard once spring arrives properly, but that will be at the expense of flowers.

For this late-summer scheme, however, I prefer to employ the dark-leaved dahlias, and there are many to choose from. Two classic varieties with star quality can never be discounted: 'Bishop of Llandaff' and its seedling offspring 'David Howard' both flower early enough to be used now. Even if they were late, the dark foliage of both would suffice. The more intricate and blacker of the two is the Bishop, a lovely foliage plant that produces mid-red peony flowers as a bonus. More modern dark-leaved singles abound, including the deep-yellow 'Knock Out', bred by Keith Hammett in the rugged climate of New Zealand. The black-tinted foliage and clear yellow flowers are exceptional. Hammett has also raised the excellent 'Magenta Star' (exactly described by the name) and rich-red 'Dovegrove'. Mark Twyning at Varfell Farm in Cornwall has produced a candy-inspired collection that includes the creamy-white 'Twyning's After Eight' and the velvet-red 'Twyning's Chocolate'. All these varieties will smoulder away for you from July until late in the year.

Above: *Dahlia* 'Twyning's After Eight'.

Right: *Sambucus nigra* f. *porphyrophylla* 'Eva'.

Opposite: *Dahlia* 'David Howard' is resplendent with *Canna* 'Wyoming' at Great Dixter. This truly great dahlia embodies the summer sun.

Autumn Riches

Dahlia 'Chat Noir'.

Exploit the jewel-box richness of September light by swirling mauve and pink asters through purple and ruby-red cactus dahlias.

Something magical happens to the garden as September arrives. The evenly balanced light seems to crisp up the colours, rather than washing them out as the summer sun high overhead did. That unique light creates a jewel-box aura, so much so that many gardeners prefer September to any other month.

There's a relaxed air, too, with most of the work over for the year. Every good day is a bonus and, as we drift towards October, misty mornings and shortening days make each hour more precious. In the soft light, however, fine detail begins to appear. The tessellated petals of the early autumn crocus, *Colchicum agrippinum*, glow now. The feathery grass *Calamagrostis brachytricha* shimmers in shades of pearl and purple, and the 'caterpillars' of the pennisetums have a gossamer quality peculiar to autumn. This season is also blessed by South American tender flowers, which peak now, encouraged by shorter days. Frost-tender salvias, dahlias, cosmos, penstemons and fuchsias look at their best.

Calamagrostis brachytricha.

You must always try to position these flowers to catch the sun in the afternoon and evening, because this position offers the most flattering light.

Asters (or Michaelmas daisies) are a vital addition. They come in shades that vary between purple, pink, lavender-blue, white and almost magenta. Every gardener should aspire to find room for some of these late-flowering stars: they will delight the bees and butterflies – reason enough to include them – but also provide good foliage and intricate buds earlier in the year. This swathe of green texture lingers in the border for months, acting as a buffer for such earlier flowers as phloxes. If more gardeners concentrated on foliage and form rather than fleeting flower, borders would be much better.

Most gardeners in most gardens can successfully grow the September-flowering New England asters, labelled A. *novae-angliae*. These produce substantial woody clumps with clusters of flowers held on stiff stems. They do not need regular division, so they persist in borders for years. More importantly, they resist mildew, which is the scourge of the New York aster (A. *novi-belgii*). I favour elegant asters that reach between 1.2 and 1.5 metres (4–5 ft) in height. Dwarf forms always seem stunted to my eyes.

Solidago rugosa
'Fireworks' sets off *Aster*
'Little Carlow'.

My personal New England favourites include the lovely 'Harrington's Pink', a clear-pink aster that opens to a single flower and reaches a height of 1.5 metres (5 ft). This innocent aster literally looks as fresh as a daisy. However, if you prefer brasher strumpets, the queen of them all is the vivid-pink 'Andenken an Alma Pötschke' (1 metre/3 ft). She catches anyone's attention from afar. 'Sayer's Croft' is Alma's offspring, a lovely aster with neatly rayed purple-pink flowers. The darker purple-pink 'Primrose Upward' is another great aster, said to be descended from 'Sayer's Croft'. Less well known is 'Helen Picton' (1.2 metres/4 ft), a new purple-violet variety from the world-famous Old Court Nurseries in Worcestershire. 'Rosa Sieger' is another excellent performer, with very large heads of rose-pink flowers.

Those with moisture-retentive soil could use these asters with certain garden-worthy phloxes, including *P. paniculata* 'Blue Paradise', a deep violet-blue in evening light, and 'Franz Schubert', a pale lilac-blue with a paler edge and a darker eye. Both reach 1.2 metres (4 ft) at least, on good soil, and both would pre-empt the asters. The clear-white 'David' would probably still be going strong in September, and possibly later. 'Monica Lynden-Bell', a soft pale pink with a strong constitution, is another ace performer, but peaks in August.

Clockwise from top left: *Aster novae-angliae* 'Primrose Upward'; *A. novae-angliae* 'Andenken an Alma Pötschke'; *Phlox paniculata* 'Monica Lynden-Bell'; *P. paniculata* 'Blue Paradise'.

Phloxes demand moisture and should be watered copiously as soon as they show the first signs of stress – wilting foliage. Once you start watering you must carry on, otherwise they will suffer. Try not to splash the leaves.

If you have soil good enough to grow these phloxes, you will also be able to include named forms of *A. novi-belgii*, the New York aster. These highly bred asters suffer from mildew (a water-stress disease), so always water them in dry weather. Mulching in early summer also helps, but always do it after rain. Plant breeders succeeded in producing hundreds of

Aster novae-angliae
'Harrington's Pink' and
A. × frikartii 'Mönch'.

cultivars in the first half of the twentieth century. Certain ones rise above the others in excellence. Good doubles include the lavender-blue 'Marie Ballard', the pale-pink 'Fellowship' and the mauve-pink 'Patricia Ballard'. All are 90–120 centimetres (3–4 ft) tall and endure well.

The smaller-flowered asters add contrasting froth to the border, and their tiny buds look fine, feathery and intricate. 'Little Carlow' (nearly blue in September light) provides a cloud of tiny flowers from this month onwards, and is worthy of a place in every garden. A. *pilosus* var. *pringlei* 'Monte Cassino' (also September-flowering) has clouds of small white flowers. A. 'Coombe Fishacre' provides the same billowing effect of hundreds of flowers, this time in a soft purple-pink flecked in red. These three resemble cumulus clouds, and all can show tiny flecks of red.

The dark foliage and strong upright stems of A. *laevis* 'Calliope' (1.3 metres/4½ ft) are an October essential if you have room for this aster with large, open grey-blue flowers. I am also fond of the gentler, shorter 'Vasterival', which seems to be a miniature of 'Calliope' but softer-stemmed and much airier. Perhaps the airiest of all, however, is the American species A. *turbinellus* with its graceful grey-blue daisies. Place it next to the copper-red sprays of the

Schizostylis coccinea 'Major'.

robust *Schizostylis coccinea* 'Major', then stand back and prepare to be dazzled and charmed.

The ironweed (or vernonia) is a close relative of the aster, and most have rich-purple flowers held in a tight cluster at the top of the stem. Naming is muddled and heights vary, so grab a tall one whenever possible. Some can reach 2.5 metres (8 ft) in good soil. The single, clean-white daisies and bright-green stems of *Leucanthemella serotina* provide contrasting verticals. Never be afraid of height. As autumn progresses these giants are silhouetted against the sun and become almost luminescent. Late-flowering muddy maroon sanguisorbas (such as *Sanguisorba* 'Cangshan Cranberry') also make fantastic beacons at this time of year, and they dazzle in the September sun. If late-flowering plants need to be divided, do it as they break into growth in spring, so that they have had the winter to recover from flowering.

Asters love full sun, but the gentle Japanese anemone can be accommodated in some shade. Heights vary: some are almost stunted and others are positively willowy. The deeper pinks cast more magic than the icy lavender-pinks, but the single white *Anemone × hybrida* 'Honorine Jobert' is beguiling in the gloom. Bred by Victor Lemoine in 1851, it has never been surpassed for purity of form.

These simply structured Japanese anemones shine in August and September, but their buds hang in the border for weeks like grey seed pearls covered in spun silk. Their ultimate accessory in a simple planting scheme is the hardy fuchsia, and the purple-and-red variety 'Mrs Popple' is a lovely partner. Some Japanese anemones colonize the garden rather too well, moving and popping up somewhere other than where they were placed. Others take several years to spread by creeping. When the Scottish plant-hunter Robert Fortune first found *Anemone hupehensis* var. *japonica*, it was growing over and among graves in a cemetery in Shanghai. This wandering habit endears them to me, and it's worth having a Japanese anemone area and letting them get on with it – after all, it's a gentle invasion.

The compact double *A. hupehensis* var. *japonica* 'Pamina' is a doughty performer, producing neatly semi-double flowers in strong pink and usually reaching a height of 90–120 centimetres (3–4 ft). It could be used with such sultry sedums as *Sedum telephium* 'Purple Emperor' and the starry white floppy aster

The large blue daisies of *Aster × frikartii* 'Jungfrau' pick up the yellowing leaves of trees at Paul Picton's Old Court Garden in Worcestershire, home of the Plant Heritage National Collection of autumn-flowering asters.

(A. *divaricatus*), and mingled with cosmos and penstemons in shades of purple. *Anemone hupehensis* var. *japonica* 'Prinz Heinrich' is not as dainty in form as 'Pamina', with more ragged semi-double flowers in the same shade of strong pink, and it's a more aggressive grower. *Anemone × hybrida* 'Margarete' is also similar, although perhaps slightly shorter, and the small pink flowers have a warmer tone. Single forms I admire include A. *hupehensis* 'Bowles's Pink', which is one of those singles with pale petals interspersed at random with darker ones. This creates sparkle, and it has endured far more readily than its newer counterpart 'Hadspen Abundance', which sadly has never lived up to its second name for me.

Good plummy and mauve-toned penstemons include 'Pensham Plum Jerkum', 'Papal Purple', 'Raven', 'Blackbird' and 'Sour Grapes'. Penstemons will persist in flowering if deadheaded well into September and October, and should survive in most gardens where winters are average as long as they are left intact; cut them down in spring once new growth has begun. Take cuttings between June and August (see p. 77).

Annual plants (which are sown, flower and die in the same year) are generally early- or midsummer performers, but cosmos is an exception. It will flower in July, but is happiest in autumn, encouraged by shorter days, a trait shared by all

natives of Mexico and South America. *C. bipinnatus* has fine feathery foliage and flowers in shades of white, pink and purple-pink. There are single and more double forms, and some have quilled petals. All must be deadheaded to keep the supply of flowers going.

If you want an annual that will really add ritzy glitz at this time of the year, none is more effective than rich-red varieties of amaranthus. *A. paniculatus* 'Marvel Bronze' has dark leaves and millet-like tops that resemble a jester's cap. One or two threaded through any border of pale blues and pinks adds richness, and the pointed tails offer a good contrast in a season dominated by daisies and saucer-shaped flowers.

Most amaranthus come from tropical areas of the world, and they demand warmth in order to grow well, as does *Cleome hassleriana*, another South American flower that's useful now. Sometimes called the spider flower, because of its long stamens and claw-shaped petals, this spiny plant needs warm conditions to thrive. To grow cosmos, amaranthus and cleome, sow the seeds in spring, prick them out into pots, keep them in the warmest place you have and plant them out once the weather has really warmed up. Water well until established, then pray for a warm, sunny summer.

The dark-red heads of amaranthus keep their colour for months and can be used to pick up dahlias. For this scheme pale-pink, purple and wine-red are the colours to plant. I grow D. 'Hillcrest Royal', a magenta-pink to purple spiky cactus, and 'Orfeo', a deep-purple cactus. The Karma series includes the pale-pink 'Karma Prospero' and the purple 'Karma Lagoon'.

Verbena bonariensis
and *Dahlia* 'Wittemans
Superba' in the exotic
garden at Great Dixter.

Cleome hassleriana.

Dahlias are garden essentials because good varieties are capable of flowering non-stop from July until the first frosts. For that reason alone they should be added to late-season borders. The variety of colours (both cool and warm) allows them to be mixed into many different schemes, and this makes them very versatile. Flower forms vary from spiky cactus to neat pompom and soft waterlily. There are singles, collarettes and semi-doubles, but it must be said that the doubles last much longer as blooms than singles.

Dahlias are frost-tender, so the tubers must be stored safely in areas with cold winters. The plants are lifted at the first sign of frost, and the roots dried off and stored in dry compost before being watered and started off in March. Regular checks sometimes reveal rotting tubers, but at least some come through. Dahlias need warmth to grow well, so progress can be slow in cool springs.

Autumn Gold

Ratibida pinnata.

The daisy, with its dusky middle, reigns supreme. Frame the yellows and rust-browns with decadent wine-red flowers and foliage to create a rich brocade.

Yellow is difficult to avoid in autumn, and generally it comes in the form of a daisy. The word is a corruption of 'day's eye', which should tell you that daisies demand sun as their birthright. They positively sulk in shade and refuse to perform. Daisy flowers last for many weeks, and are greatly varied in form, from the green-coned sombrero of *Rudbeckia laciniata* 'Herbstsonne' to the tiny, neatly rayed, button-sized *Rudbeckia triloba* and the swooning *Ratibida pinnata*, which droops its petals throughout the day like a lady in great distress.

The central cone is the business end of each daisy: it contains a collection of tiny flowers, and the nectar and pollen from within these satisfy pollinating insects. The colourful ray petals that we admire so much are simply decorative. Many daisies drop them after a few weeks but keep their cone, and these 'bobbles' provide another season of interest. I love the tall, self-supporting stems of 'Herbstsonne' once the petals drop to reveal a series of olive-green, acorn-shaped cones.

Helianthus 'Lemon Queen'.

The heights, sizes and stance of daisies also vary, and not all are mound-formers. Some provide uprights, some egg-shaped ovals and some a floating sea of flowers. Many chase the sun round the garden, so try not to position them so that you spend most of your time looking at the back of the flower. If you can look into the sun between midday and three when you view your border, your daisies will probably be copying you, keeping their backs to you as they worship the sun.

There are certain yellow daisies that are far too pushy and which I could never recommend: among them are *Helianthus* 'Miss Mellish' and 'Gullick's Variety'. Anyone who has ever grown either will know that they are both capable of colonizing a large area in one season, smothering everything in their wake. They have foot-shaped roots and they will walk all over you. These are the plants that the late Graham Stuart Thomas (British plantsman extraordinaire) described as 'bright yellow, coarse and rough'.

However, that could never be said about *Helianthus* 'Lemon Queen'. It is tall (1.5–1.8 metres/5–6 ft) but self-supporting, with a tight clump-forming habit, and sends up hundreds of pallid yellow daisies, which hang in the air like small spinning plates for many weeks, their centres finely flecked with blackish brown. This is a plant I have grown for decades; it always wins plaudits, and has an impeccable pedigree. It was raised by Thomas Carlile of the Loddon Nursery in Twyford, near Reading in Berkshire, between 1940 and 1950. Carlile seems to have adored yellow daisies: he also raised the golden-yellow single *Heliopsis helianthoides* var. *scabra* 'Light of Loddon' (1.4 metres/4½ ft) and the slightly ragged golden-yellow double *Helianthus* 'Loddon Gold' (2 metres/6½ ft).

The tall lemon-yellow *Ratibida pinnata*, with its drooping lemon-yellow petals, is another favourite of mine. It is easy to grow and keeps itself in a tight clump, but it does need staking. I run an almost no-stake garden, but peonies and *R. pinnata* are the exceptions. I love the latter's long stems and languid flowers, but most of all I am fascinated by their dusky, bumpy brown thimbles. The flowers can appear as early as late July, but those thimbles keep me interested until autumn.

For most of the year I would always choose a pallid yellow in favour of a brassy one. The cooler lemon-yellows are fresh and youthful, and they don't jump out at you. They position themselves like a spinning thread – gleaming rather than glaring. However, once autumn descends it's the stronger, brasher yellows that work a special magic in the border. They add an ornate richness, a decadence that is welcome as the

A soft golden mixture
of rudbeckia among
the upright grass
Calamagrostis × acutiflora
'Karl Foerster' fades
into autumn.

year is waning. Somehow the lower sun picks up their colour
to greater effect.

Few daisies endure as long in flower as the Gloriosas,
varieties bred from *Rudbeckia hirta*. They will overwinter, but
most gardeners treat them as annuals. There are many named
forms: some are stunted and rather unattractive, and others
have green middles, making them difficult to place; the bright-
yellow single ones with brown centres are the easiest to grow.
My own favourite is the large-rayed 'Indian Summer', which
produces flat-topped flowers 15–20 centimetres (6–8 in.) in
diameter. Their almost black centres have a Fibonacci spiral in
the middle, and this clean-cut daisy is more than eye-catching.

Most of the single-flowered bright-yellow daisies have
brown cones and dark centres. The way to use them, should
you be especially nervous of their loud colour, is to balance
them with dark foliage, sultry reds or strong, dark blues, or
all three together. This contrast makes golden yellow stand
out in a proper context. One of the best ways of adding the
mysterious dark element is to plant a dark-leaved cotinus,
such as *C. coggygria* 'Royal Purple'. This keeps its maroon-red
lollipop leaves late, and cold weather will often add a touch
of vivid pink to the edges. It's one of the few shrubs I use in
herbaceous planting, and it picks up the sombre middles of

daisies, enhances plummy grasses and turns strong yellows into something tasteful. You could equally use the dark *Amaranthus paniculatus* 'Marvel Bronze' or the red-leaved *Atriplex hortensis* var. *rubra* (both annuals). Dark-leaved dahlias would also work.

Dark blue is always in short supply, like hen's teeth, but the two true-blue perennial plants I would recommend are the rich-blue monkshood *Aconitum carmichaelii* 'Arendsii' and *Strobilanthes wallichii* (formerly *S. atropurpureus*). The former is a strong aconitum with stiff, downy stems that don't flag, shiny green leaves and substantial monkshood flowers. Its strong colour makes it simply the best of the later-flowering aconitums. *S. wallichii* is a variable plant, but a very good 1.2-metre-high (4 ft) form with large violet-blue flowers is sold under that name. Further touches of blue can be achieved by growing the frost-tender *Salvia guaranitica* (the anise-scented sage), which flowers usefully late, although those in colder climates will have to protect it from frost and take it inside during the winter. This woody sage grows best in a little shade, producing substantial dark-blue flowers held in dark calices. One of the best varieties is 'Black and Blue'.

Overcome your long-held prejudices and try to use goldenrod, because its curving flower heads provide a

Above: *Cotinus coggygria* 'Royal Purple'.

Right: *Aconitum carmichaelii* 'Arendsii'.

complete contrast in form to everything else. The best is the September-flowering *Solidago rugosa* 'Fireworks', which provides a sheath of stems topped by yellow flowers. It is interesting for months before it flowers, a fountain of greenish-yellow buds in waiting.

Finally, there are two curious annuals that share a sunny disposition. The Mexican hat flower, *Ratibida columnifera*, is a warm-season wild flower with orange, yellow and brown flowers. The petals droop round the tall central cone like a limp skirt. The divided foliage is glaucous, a good clue that this is a sun-lover. The whole plant reaches 60 centimetres (2 ft) and flops and climbs through the border, emerging now and again. It's easy to grow and can come through the winter. *Ipomoea lobata* (formerly *Mina lobata*) is a climbing plant known as Spanish flag for its sunny combination of yellow and red. The flowers are in subtle shades, though, and cream-apricot creeps into them, so it's warm rather than brash. The stalks are dark and wiry, and the long flowers tremble and move well above the stem. The joy of this plant is that it begins to flower in summer and lingers late into the year. It is perfect for a tripod, especially a rusty iron one; it performs in sun and shade and is more floriferous on a poor diet.

Opposite: A late-summer bed of daylily, *Verbena bonariensis*, *Helenium autumnale* and *Rudbeckia hirta* Gloriosa Mixed.

Above: *Ratibida columnifera* 'Red Midget'.

Right: *Ipomoea lobata*.

Autumn Canvas

Grasses add movement
as they fade. Here, a
mixture of *Miscanthus
sinensis* 'Silberfeder'
and *Cortaderia selloana*
'Pumila' fountains up.

As the mists swirl through autumn, the garden fades, but low sun spotlights late-season silver and gold grasses, adding movement, while others are reduced to skeletons standing stiff and rigid.

The essentials at this time of year are well-behaved grasses, ones that don't self-seed or stray willy-nilly across the plot. They offer a great deal as autumn fades into winter. They move, they sway, they rumba to the music that this season plays as the year wanes; they catch the raindrop pearls and hold the frost and, as the heads disintegrate, they form a gossamer veil of gold and silver. The taller ones offer vital vertical accents and link the garden with the sky above, breaking up the floral monopoly of daisies. The ground-hugging grasses either spiral out like anemones on the seabed or toss their golden hair in the wind like a lover spurned. Threaded through an area, grasses unite the planting scheme. However, it's vital to place them where they can sparkle in the sun, otherwise the detail is lost in gloom. In any case, many need warm conditions in order to rise into growth.

The warm, faded presence of those grasses that turn the colour of bleached canvas is just the ticket when it comes to

Above: *Verbena bonariensis*.

Opposite, top: *Calamagrostis × acutiflora* 'Karl Foerster'.

Opposite, bottom: Gradually these grasses, *Molinia caerulea* subsp. *arundinacea* 'Karl Foerster' and *Miscanthus sinensis* 'Rotsilber', will fade to mink-brown and bleached canvas.

showing off late flowers that might include the tall, willowy *Verbena bonariensis* or the shorter *V. rigida*. The latter reaches only 30 centimetres (1 ft) or so in height, but its punchy purple flowers are much more vibrant than those of the more popular but duller *V. bonariensis*. *V. rigida* forms a branching candelabra that is always topped by yet another flower, as though a magician were pulling them from a hat. They appear like jewels in a sea of pale-gold grasses. *V. bonariensis* is still desirable for its height (1–2 metres/3–6 ft) and mauve-purple domes of flower, and it has a tensile strength that allows it to resist the weather. Eventually it forms a black seed head of small diamonds; seedlings may follow.

As the year fades these rakish plants die beautifully, like Adonis stretched on a couch in a Pre-Raphaelite painting. It is so much better than having a bare, 'put-to-bed' garden – for you and for wildlife. I do not advocate a dedicated grass border for most of us, but if I had a huge garden I would probably plant one. Whatever you do, don't include just one or two specimens. The minimum number is three, and they should be placed carefully to balance the border.

One of the most effective grasses for a tall vertical sheath of stems fittingly bears Karl Foerster's name. This German nurseryman and landscape architect (1874–1970) forged a new

style of planting (long before Piet Oudolf made it popular), and showed us how to use grasses or 'nature's hair', as he preferred to call them. By October the feather reed grass (*Calamagrostis × acutiflora* 'Karl Foerster') stretches up its wand-like stems as no other grass does as it reaches for the sky. It provides a presence for months, firstly with its vivid-green spring foliage, then in summer with purple-flushed awns that soon turn to wheaten gold, but I value it for its winter sheath of russet-brown stems. I have planted other forms, including the variegated, vertically striped cream-and-green 'Overdam' and the newer 'Avalanche' (both about 1 metre/3 ft), but neither have endured into winter with any conviction, so I have returned to Karl. It's easy to grow for all, forms a tight clump and never sets seed. Plant it, then stand back and admire it. One positioned well will work alone; using three spaced out is also good; but planting just two is wrong. I have also seen it planted in swathes to great effect.

The most majestic of the taller grasses is *Miscanthus sinensis*, which flutters over the garden as imperiously as the royal standard lording it above Buckingham Palace. It appears late, however, and the flowering time is later the further north you are in the northern hemisphere. My Cotswold garden, for instance, is high and bleak, and I rarely see my miscanthus in

flower before September. Some wait until October, others flower not at all. It is frustrating that not far to the south miscanthus flowers by mid-July – some six weeks earlier. The earliest to flower is an older variety called 'Silberfeder': it is often written off by those whose geographical position makes them lucky enough to have a greater choice. Use it as a litmus paper, to see how you go. Most miscanthus have mid-green leaves with a central pale stripe, so all is not lost if they fail to flower.

These late-season grasses (*M. sinensis*) have evolved from a species found in the lowlands and mountains of Japan, Korea and China, which experience a summer rainy season lasting roughly six weeks, when days of heavy, torrential rain are interrupted by bursts of warmth. This is perfect growing weather, and those with good soil will always do better with miscanthus. Their plants will be taller and more luscious. Whatever your soil, though, newly planted ones will take at least three years to form a good clump.

In the cooler parts of the northern hemisphere miscanthus doesn't set seed, but the German nurseryman Ernst Pagels (1913–2007) managed to coax *M. sinensis* 'Graziella' (a fluffy, silvery cultivar) into producing a seed crop by growing it under heated glass over winter. The resulting seedlings were pleasingly variable, and several Pagels varieties have become garden classics, all at about 1.6 metres (5¼ ft) tall. 'Ferner Osten' produces tightly formed purple-pink awns with white tips. It is surely the most vivid miscanthus of all, but the heads will fade to mink-brown within four weeks. 'Flamingo' flowers three weeks earlier, but the rose-pink to purple awns are floppier and airier. I prefer 'Ferner Osten'. 'Malepartus' is another early red, but I have found it less robust than 'Ferner Osten'. Those who can grow 'Malepartus' well always treasure it. 'Kaskade' lives up to its name, producing drooping silky flowers in silver-pink. Of the silvers, the tall 'Silberfeder' (selected by Hans Simon in the early 1950s) still holds its own, sending out lots of flowers that reach between 2 and 3 metres (6½–10 ft) in height.

Some miscanthus varieties are grown for their variegated foliage, and the tradition of using striped miscanthus to cast light and shade was employed by Gertrude Jekyll and William Robinson more than a hundred years ago. They knew them as *Eulalia japonica* and used a form now called *M. sinensis* 'Zebrinus', or zebra grass, a favourite plant of Japanese gardeners. This graceful but substantial grass is horizontally banded in gold, but it has an arching habit that some find difficult. 'Strictus' is more erect, but less graceful. Both reach 1.6 metres (5¼ ft), going to 2 metres (6½ ft) once (and if) they

flower. I prefer the subtler variegation of Pagels's 'Pünktchen', and this does flower a little for me in late October.

Another old Japanese form, 'Morning Light', is a more delicate affair, with fine leaves vertically striped in white and banded in cream. It provides a good sheath of foliage in smaller gardens, but flowers for me only in exceptional summers, and then the flowers are rather wispy and inconspicuous. It reaches only 1 metre (3 ft) in height in my garden, yet it should be twice as tall. If you are after a compact miscanthus for flower, use 'Yakushima Dwarf', a finely leaved grass that produces masses of upright cockades of mink-brown flowers that barely rise above the foliage. Its rounded form makes it a very good specimen plant.

Much brasher variegated forms include M. *sinensis* var. *condensatus* 'Cabaret' and 'Cosmopolitan' (both 2 metres/6½ ft). Both have pale-green leaves that are barcoded longitudinally in white and cream. 'Cosmopolitan', the bolder of the two, has white edges to the green leaves. 'Cabaret', thought to be less hardy, has cream edges to green-striped leaves. I have found both trying to grow – they survive in my garden, rather than shine – but I persevere, and place them near tall, red monardas.

Varieties of M. *sinensis* will keep a flowery presence in the border until late January, but then they should be cut back

Molinia caerulea subsp. arundinacea 'Windspiel'.

hard to ground level to allow the new growth to appear from the base. It must be done early, because the new growth emerges inside the old stems early in the year. Some gardeners (including the designer Dan Pearson) don't cut miscanthus back at all, but I like it to start afresh.

Karl Foerster also developed several tall molinias, differentiated from the shorter purple moor grasses (*M. caerulea*) by the addition of the subspecies *arundinacea*. These tall grasses give a presence late into the year, but fail to endure into January. Their foliage often colours up to a warm honey-brown or gold. The flowering heads vary from finely beaded to plume-like, and heights vary, too, with some reaching 2–3 metres (6–10 ft). The most finely beaded of all is 'Transparent' (2 metres/6 ft), and the true form should develop airy heads of tiny beads that darken almost to black. These jet beads look stunning in low light. The slightly shorter 'Bergfreund' (1.5 metres/5 ft) is similar in flower form, but with brown heads held above yellow leaves; it stands out well. 'Karl Foerster' is also highly desirable for its erect branching heads, stems and foliage. These turn rust-orange as the temperatures drop, picking up the colour of orange-toned dahlias (such as 'David Howard') and any golden daisies still battling on. 'Skyracer' is upright, probably the tallest at over 2 metres (6 ft), and this grass also colours up to gold from tip to toe.

The most substantial head belongs to 'Windspiel', a grass named after its habit of swaying in the wind. Molinias need good light and they prefer rich soil. They create a different profile from miscanthus, because their foliage tends to curve outwards (like a large tussock) and the long, slender stems rise well above, veering out at a slight angle. A mature clump can be covered in flowers.

Shorter grasses can be equally useful, and many give an all-year presence. The ubiquitous pony-tail grass (*Stipa tenuissima*) gives a candyfloss texture late in the year as it trembles through late, dark penstemons. And because it turns harvest gold in early summer, rather than waiting until autumn, you can thread it under the slender drumstick

Stipa tenuissima;
S. tenuissima and Allium
sphaerocephalon.

allium (A. *sphaerocephalon*) and through such flat-topped achilleas as 'Walther Funcke', which is a deliciously earthy shade of orange-brown. In common with many stipas, this is a warm-season grass that demands hot sun and good drainage whenever possible. Hardiness has never been a problem, although it will not like cold, wet clay. There is a similar but even hardier stipa – S. *lessingiana*, commonly called the Russian steppe grass – that may be slightly taller. It is very tough and creates the same effect as S. *tenuissima*.

Two more substantial stipas flower earlier in the year. Although both have largely disintegrated by autumn, both have star quality and should be recognized. The easiest to grow and place is *Stipa gigantea,* the golden oat grass, which fountains out in June. The low mound of grey-green foliage allows many other plants to grow close by, and the golden-brown awns constantly tremble and shake, providing a wonderful gauzy veil for months. By October all that remains is a series of fine strands. *Stipa barbata*, a native of North Africa and southern Europe, needs a warm position in order to produce its 30-centimetre-long (1 ft) ostrich-feather awns. These emerge as flowing silk before drying off to produce gossamer strands that catch the light. Few plants offer such

Panicum virgatum
'Rubrum'; *Achillea*
'Walther Funcke'.

movement or luminosity in summer sun: sometimes it seems
to be doing breaststroke in the border, at others it flicks its
hair like a horse swatting flies with its tail. The mesmerizing
sight ends when the sharply pointed awns detach themselves
and corkscrew into the ground, usually by August. S. *barbata*
is short-lived, however, and difficult to grow from seeds
collected from the plant.

Panicums also enjoy warmth, and given the right
conditions forms of *Panicum virgatum* will thrive, producing
clouds of pink- or purple-toned spikelets. Varieties can be
grouped by type. Some are grown for their colourful autumn
foliage and others for their clouds of tiny flowers. Grey-leaved
forms include 'Heavy Metal', 'Northwind' and 'Prairie Sky',
and these are grown for that stainless-steel colour that
flatters cool-spectrum purples, blues and pinks. 'Heavy Metal'
is the most upright, reaching almost 1.5 metres (5 ft). The
top coating of pink awns contrasts well with the blue foliage.
'Northwind' is taller and the panicles are small, but the
sheath of leaves forms a dense clump, eventually colouring
to yellow in autumn. These blue-leaved forms can fail to
colour up in cooler areas.

Karl Foerster's early selection 'Rotstrahlbusch' (red ray
bush) was selected for its autumn colour. Newer varieties that

A simple planting of the drought-tolerant *Hydrangea arborescens* 'Annabelle' and the hardiest pennisetum, *P. alopecuroides* 'Hameln', will endure for months.

develop this wine-red tone include 'Shenandoah', probably the most colourful of all panicums. 'Squaw' (which has green leaves and pink flowers) also develops rich-red leaves, and is said to be better than 'Warrior', a purpler-flowered form with reddish-brown leaves in autumn. The heights of these will vary according to growing conditions, and many that are said to grow to 1.5 metres (5 ft) in North America will probably reach only 1 metre (3 ft) in northern Europe. 'Cloud Nine' is the tallest, a small-flowered variety that turns golden-yellow. The ones with noticeable foliage should be given space to shine, but those with airy panicles look handsome popping up among late-summer perennials.

Pennisetums also thrive in warmer gardens on well-drained soil. Their excellent mound of fine grey-green foliage and soft fluffy 'caterpillars' look at their best at the front of the border. There are pink-flowered forms, of which 'Karley Rose' is the earliest, but the most handsome have woolly flower heads in beige and brown. In more exposed gardens these will arrive late, but they are worth waiting for.

The hardiest (and therefore the most sensible option) is *P. alopecuroides* 'Hameln'. It is the most reliable in cooler districts, with green foliage and flowers that eventually turn golden-brown. But anyone who can should grow those with darker tails in black and purple, including 'Black Beauty' and 'Moudry'. They reach 60 centimetres (2 ft) in height, and flop and curtsey on a sunny day like cats waiting to be stroked. Nursery owners sell them in autumn – not the best time to plant a dubiously tender plant. Late spring is when they should go in, and this is also the time to cut back any pennisetums you have overwintered.

I have successfully overwintered two pennisetums for many years in ordinary winters. *P. macrourum* (1.8 metres/6 ft) has long, slender flower heads that resemble finger-length pipe cleaners, held on long stems that fountain outwards. It flowers earlier than most. The fluffy-tailed *P. villosum* (80 centimetres/ 2½ ft), with its off-white, angora-soft heads, is the most tactile of all pennisetums. It can survive as a perennial, although that depends on good drainage. I find these highly touchable grasses soften the border edges brilliantly.

It doesn't matter to me that pennisetums and panicums flower late; there's something wonderful about knowing that there are still plants 'in waiting' on a crisp autumn day. I am also fond of a short calamagrostis that appears in late summer: *C. brachytricha.* It produces intricate heads in pearl-pink (like small feather dusters), which obligingly pop up in shade or sun. This cool-pink-to-grey mother-of-pearl colour matches asters, late-flowering sedums and all the other grasses. It is a useful and reliable addition.

The best flowering perennials for this scheme inject flashes of sombre-toned colour at lower levels, and the later-flowering sedums are stiff-stemmed and enduring. The ordinary *S. spectabile* is silver-pink, but the hybrid

Calamagrostis brachytricha
is a low-growing billower
that can be used to
frame a path or border.

S. 'Herbstfreude' (formerly 'Autumn Joy') begins life as a vision of bright pink before its starry flowers turn chocolate-brown. 'Matrona' ('matronly') is a plump, robust vision of metallic pigeon-grey and pink – a Goliath of the plant world. The much darker and more compact 'Karfunkelstein' and 'Purple Emperor' also add darker glints of colour. The almost perpetual double-flowered *Salvia nemorosa* 'Pusztaflamme' has the same moody blue presence, and lasts for months. Newer green- or grey-leaved sedums of the collectable kind include the bright-pink 'Cloud Walker' and 'Mr Goodbud', which has wide clusters of purple-pink flowers that stay late.

Eupatorium maculatum 'Riesenschirm' matches the tallest grasses for scale, with stiff, dark stems of whorled leaves topped by fluffy 20-centimetre-wide (8 in.) heads of moody purple to pink flowers. These hover 2.4 metres (8 ft) above the ground, attracting butterflies and picking up the colour of toning grasses, including *Miscanthus sinensis* 'Ferner Osten'. By October the flowers have become a dark chocolate hue. The taller monardas are also stiff-stemmed enough to provide a contrast with grasses. *Monarda* 'Scorpion' produces pinkish-purple flowers that emerge from a pepper-pot head in summer. The bracts supporting the flowers are

Sedum 'Herbstfreude';
S. telephium 'Purple
Emperor'.

a deep sooty purple, but by the time the grasses are in full
autumn flow the monarda has turned into a burnt-wood
plant sculpture, and it will stand through winter. It is one
of the woodiest herbaceous plants on offer.

Once the highlights are added the autumn canvas can
be left to mirror the vagaries of the weather. One day it
will look sooty and sombre, another it will take on the
patina of weathered oak. When a sparkling frost descends
the mood will change again, and that is when this type
of planting excels.

Winter Festivities

Winter is the season when evergreens matter. Here, *Pyrus salicifolia* 'Pendula' is encircled by box domes.

Although winter strips much of the garden bare, evergreen foliage glows. If the leaves are high-gloss green and there's a glimmer of red, it's a winter warmer.

Whenever you are lucky enough to be a passenger in winter in a cross-country car journey that traverses hill and dale, make sure you gaze around. This season clears the decks and opens up the landscape to reveal every contour and cranny. This happens in the garden on a lesser scale: the ferns in the hidden depths take a giant leap forwards, and you can sense their bristled stems and intricate fronds from afar; the box topiary that buried itself in the froth of the flower border for much of the year becomes crisp, strong and prominent; and yew hedges start to dominate, rather than frame. Walls, gates and paving suddenly show their texture and, although the garden is largely devoid of flowers, those rich shafts of green mean that it doesn't matter. Green is not an option, it's a necessity.

This strong infusion of glossy winter evergreens is warm and consoling, so it's not surprising that our ancestors revered the Green Man for his power and promise of rebirth. Garden

The berries of *Cotoneaster frigidus* 'Cornubia'.

The berries of *Cotoneaster frigidus* 'Cornubia'.

designers seem to share that sense of pagan worship, although modern practitioners (such as Arne Maynard and Piet Oudolf) have veered away from the straight lines of the traditional parterre. Instead, cloud-pruned box, plump collections of hummocks in varying sizes and slender Loch Ness monsters mimic the landscape.

The lipstick touches of red are the cherry on the winter cake, bringing the garden alive in the shape of fruit and berry. They lure in the birds, and that creates a conflict for gardeners because some berries (including those of the holly) are always picked off as the shortest day approaches. Others are taken only in severe weather; they include *Cotoneaster frigidus* 'Cornubia', a large tree-like shrub that can keep its red clusters of fruit until March. Personally I love to see gorging birds stripping the fruit away as winter bites. My pair of binoculars becomes a desk essential.

Of the most reliable and popular evergreens, box suits smaller areas much more than yew, which is a far larger plant. There are many different forms, but the best for clipping into a tight shape is the widely available *Buxus sempervirens*. You can clip it into formal cones, pyramids or roundels, fashion it into hedges or make organic shapes to suit yourself. Ready-topiarized shapes can be bought: I am the proud owner of a

Rosemary Verey's
famous box parterre
at Barnsley House in
Gloucestershire is in an
elaborate pattern, but a
simpler design would
still enhance winter.

box hen and cockerel, and I love them both dearly. The fun element of topiary should not be underestimated, and HRH Prince Charles's Gloucestershire garden, Highgrove, has large chess pieces cut from golden yews that used to be plain puddings.

When buying box, try to find specimens grown in airy conditions rather than muggy plastic tunnels, because the fungal disease box blight (*Cylindrocladium buxicola*) is far more likely to thrive in airless conditions under cover. It will defoliate your plants and look obviously fungal, showing black lesions, before spreading to other box plants.

For this reason alone, taking your own cuttings is desirable. This can be done in late summer and early autumn. Collect new 10-centimetre (4-in.) sprigs from mature, healthy-looking plants, trim them beneath a leaf node and plunge them into small pots containing half-and-half horticultural sand and compost. Pot them up in the following spring and plant out when well rooted. If you want a hedge, leave 30 centimetres (1 ft) between plants. For a roundel, plant five or six cuttings in a 25-centimetre (9-in.) circle. Clip box in early June, after the fear of frost has passed. If it needs a second trim, to keep an extra-neat profile through winter, clip it again lightly in early September.

Yew and box are both long-lived, but yew (*Taxus baccata*) has incorrectly gained a reputation for being extremely slow-growing. It is possible to get a yew hedge of substance within eight years if you plant it in enriched ground. Buy bare-root whips and plant between November and March, leaving 50-centimetre (18-in.) gaps. Plant only in clement weather, never in freezing conditions. Feed the plants fortnightly throughout the growing season with a nitrogen-rich plant food, starting in spring. In the early stages, trim your young yew hedge two or three times during the growing season to make it bushier. However, resist the urge to lop the top until the desired height is reached. An unlopped yew hedge will put on 40 centimetres (15 in.) of growth a year, but a topped one loses that urge to put on height. It grows outwards instead, and takes much longer to reach the desired height.

Yew has one large advantage over most other conifers: it can regenerate from bare wood, so you can manage its size. Once established, yew needs an annual trim, but the growth

Ilex aquifolium
'Handsworth New Silver';
I. aquifolium 'Argentea
Marginata'.

can be sappy. If you are using shears (for topiary, for instance) a bucket of water, scrubbing brush and cloth are useful. Immerse the blades in water, scrub them and wipe with a damp cloth regularly – this helps you to get a clean cut. It's also useful to lay down a large sheet or tarpaulin to catch the clippings. Always try to cut yew on a dull day, or when the foliage has a covering of dew, to prevent sun scorch. Feed with blood, fish and bone after cutting.

Smaller choice evergreen shrubs to add to yew and box could include *Sarcococca confusa*, *Daphne laureola* (see p. 25) and *Skimmia* × *confusa* 'Kew Green'. The last is the finest of the skimmias because it forms small lilac-like heads of tight green buds in the autumn, months before it opens its creamy, scented flowers – giving half a year of interest.

Holly is much slower-growing than yew, but the berries and leafy profile are among the best. Variegation is common. Golden variegation will brighten and warm a dull corner, naturally toning with warm yellows, oranges and blues. Silver variegation has a cooler presence and will flatter pinks and purples. Pricklier hollies (varieties of *Ilex aquifolium*) should not be added to borders unless you have a masochistic streak. Good green-leaved varieties include *I. aquifolium* 'Alaska', a dense, compact holly with spiny green leaves,

Ilex × altaclerensis
'Golden King'.

paler undersides and dark-red berries. It clips well into topiary and cloud-pruned hedges. Other hollies could be cut into wedding cakes, cones and roundels. 'Madame Briot' is a prickly French holly with jaunty butter-yellow-and-green leaves topped with vivid-red berries. 'Handsworth New Silver' berries well, and the birds tend to leave them. Its crisp, dark leaves are finely edged in pale cream. 'Argentea Marginata' produces large clusters of red berries set against dark-olive leaves neatly edged in cream, and grows into a fine pyramidal specimen tree given time.

Fortunately there are hardy hybrids with larger, rounder, kinder-on-the-hands foliage – Highclere holly or *Ilex × altaclerensis* – although the females (see below) do tend to produce fewer berries. The purple stems of the large 'Camelliifolia', a plain-green berrying form, are magnificent in winter light. 'Golden King' has green leaves edged with a broad irregular band of custard-yellow. It can be clipped and, although it does not berry well, the birds leave the berries as a last resort.

Most hollies are dioecious: they have male flowers on one bush and females on another. In order to get berries you must have male pollen for the ladies, but just one male can service a harem of ladies. Note that names don't always indicate the correct sex; 'Golden King', for instance, is a female berrier.

Finally, scatter some red fruits over the green of your garden by growing one or both of these choice trees: *Malus × robusta* 'Red Sentinel' and *Cotoneaster* 'Hybridus

Malus × robusta 'Red Sentinel'.

Pendulus'. The former is a healthy, scab-resistant crab apple that produces an abundance of white blossom followed by round fruits that turn in colour from Cox's orange pippin to lipstick pink. More importantly, the fruits, which look stunning against bare wood, linger late. I am not a cotoneaster fan – who is? – but the small tree 'Hybridus Pendulus' is a cracker. It reaches barely 2 metres (6 ft) and produces a tight mass of weeping branches that stay evergreen in mild winters. Think of it as semi-evergreen, and imagine a green umbrella jewelled in red: warming winter colour at its best.

Winter Sugar and Spice

Hamamelis × intermedia
'Aphrodite'.

The winter solstice sees the days begin to stretch out once more, and the first flowers are subtle treasures of soft colour with an added bonus: some are sweetly scented.

There's a wonderful moment in winter when you realize that the garden is resurfacing after its annual sleep. The days are a little longer, the sun has crept over the roof once again and warmed more of the soil, the sedum shoots are up (like miniature succulents) and the bright-red spears of the peony are nudging above the ground.

These are signs of things to come, and a tide of optimism begins to course through the gardener's veins. Yet there are only a few winter flowers that manage to perform during the first few weeks of the year, and these need to be carefully placed in shelter near the house. These winter gems are not at all showy. Most are pallid, and I think of them as frosted sugared almonds and candied peel with their tiny white, yellow-orange or pale-pink flowers. For all their pallor they stand out well in steely winter light, when there is little competition.

The sugar-and-spice season starts for me when the sweetly scented lilac-pink flowers of *Daphne bholua* 'Jacqueline Postill'

Helleborus orientalis with peony buds.

peek out from their evergreen, almond-shaped leaves. If there is a faintly warm January afternoon the first bumble-bee queens will emerge, too (always *Bombus terrestris*), and it isn't long before they find the *Daphne* flowers for an aperitif to the spring feast ahead. Occasionally, if it's warm enough, the scent wafts divinely through the air.

'Jacqueline Postill' is my desert-island daphne: the one I would take when pressed to make a choice from ten. I want everyone to enjoy it. This special plant arose as a seedling at Hillier Nurseries in Hampshire in 1982. It was noticeably different, and Alan Postill, the propagator, named it after his wife. It is unique in being the only truly evergreen form of *D. bholua*, a Himalayan species that is usually deciduous or semi-deciduous. In the wild, the higher the altitude the more deciduous the species becomes. The appropriately named *D. bholua* var. *glacialis* 'Gurkha' is a deciduous form collected and introduced in 1962. It flowers on bare stems and is equally scented, but it isn't nearly as sumptuous as Jacqueline, with her lavish foliage backing ice-pink flowers.

Good daphnes are difficult to find in almost every respect. They are difficult to propagate and slow to get to a commercial size; this makes them expensive, and gardeners are reluctant to pay for them. A well-grown one should be skilfully grafted.

Look for the graft union, normally 10–15 centimetres (4–6 in.) above ground level, and check that it is sound and clean. Try to buy a flowering plant, and once it's planted, don't prune it and don't move it unless you are prepared to risk losing it.

Even if you treat your daphnes wonderfully well, they can still be capricious. Whenever your garden contains a daphne at the height of her powers, plant another, for rather like a bride on her wedding day she will never be quite as good again. Death comes without warning and it can be sudden.

Scent has a powerful effect on the emotions and, if you can find a sheltered corner of your garden, you will get a waft of perfume to lift your spirits in the depths of winter, just when you need it most. After all, gardening is sensuous and creative. The highest accolade for scent must go to the evergreen *Sarcococca hookeriana* var. *digyna*. The stamens are red-pink and the greenish-yellow foliage has the metallic gleam you find on stressed olive trees. It's not an attractive combination. Consequently I prefer the shiny true-green leaves and ivory anthers of *S. confusa*, which can be grown in a container close to a doorway, or in a sheltered nook near a gate or door. There is scent even on cool days.

Snowdrops also appear now. The earliest often have *plicatus* blood, a term that means 'pleated'. Examine the leaves

Clockwise from left:
Narcissus 'Cedric Morris';
Galanthus plicatus 'Three
Ships'; G. 'Titania'.

carefully and you will see that the outer edges at the base
have a tiny sliver folded back on the margins. The leaves are
wide and blunt and vary in colour. Some are almost striped
in blue-green; others are substantial and green. Plicate
snowdrops tend to form larger bulbs than the northern
European native, *Galanthus nivalis*, and the flowers have
thickly textured white petals that resemble seersucker. The
inner markings are often in the form of a cross, although not
always. 'Three Ships', a fine example of a plicate, is so early
that it often flowers by Christmas Day – hence the name.

The 20-centimetre-high (8 in.), pallid-yellow *Narcissus*
'Cedric Morris' is a diminutive charmer early in the year,
bridging winter and spring. It was collected in about 1920
from the roadside in Spain, by the East Anglian artist and
plantsman for whom it is named. Its small canary-yellow
flowers hang their heads a little, and are shaded in green on
the backs of the petals; it will flower in shade or sun. It's more
inclined to flower early in a hot spot, though, which is where
the sharp-eyed Morris found it, but it has not been seen in
the wild since.

If you have a south-facing wall, use it to cosset a fine
form of the winter-flowering clematis: *C. cirrhosa* var. *balearica*.
Often referred to as the fern-leaved clematis, because of its

dark, divided foliage, this twiner will produce ivory bells lightly spotted in maroon. It's much subtler than *C. cirrhosa* var. *purpurascens* 'Freckles', which has cream bells heavily dappled in a brighter red, although 'Freckles' flowers earlier. Both will please the bees enormously and both will scramble around doors and windows, allowing you to peer up into the flowers. No pruning is required, just a gentle tidy after flowering if necessary.

These are two flowers that make winter more bearable, and the winter-flowering iris (*I. unguicularis*) provides a perfect skirt in front of them. Pointed buds open to reveal translucent flowers in soft blues and mauves. These flat-topped flowers bask in winter sun, popping up in ones and twos from November onwards and finishing with a mass flourish in April.

If you have room in an area of the garden that gets some sunshine, add a witch hazel. They come in shades of citrus-yellow, marmalade-orange, butterscotch-brown and spicy paprika-red, and weave through the garden like winter spiders casting a magic web, providing highlights that flicker. The best on offer are hybrids between Asian and American species: varieties of *Hamamelis* × *intermedia*. These have longer ribbons and more colourful calices. 'Jelena' is a particularly good copper-orange form with colourful autumn foliage that turns crimson by the end of September. Others drop their leaves quickly in autumn to reveal the promising fists of buds clustered close to bare branches.

Iris unguicularis 'Mary Barnard'.

Clematis cirrhosa var. *balearica*.

Opposite, clockwise from top left: *Hamamelis × intermedia* 'Aphrodite'; *H. × intermedia* 'Strawberries and Cream'; *H. × intermedia* 'Harry'; *H. × intermedia* 'Aurora'.

Above: *Hamamelis × intermedia* 'Jelena'.

The lovely 'Aphrodite' is a slightly scented orange-red of great vibrance. The paler orange 'Harry' is more spidery, with a slight scent. 'Aurora' produces a dull-gold ribbon from a purple calyx; not everyone likes its muddier colour, but the freesia scent makes it an essential in my garden. Buds are set only in areas where wood can ripen in warm sunshine, and it's quite possible to have flowers on one half of a bush and not on the other, if it has been shaded. Witch hazels like deep, fertile soil but do not demand acid conditions. They enjoy clay, too, but they do need water in the growing season (between June and September). Tip two or three buckets over your plant every week in dry summers until the rains come – that's the way to produce flowers. Pepper these through your garden in your most sheltered spots, and winter will be so much more bearable.

Winter Primaries

Iris reticulata.

Jaunty colours brave the start of the year as the annual battle between winter and spring takes place. Bright yellow dominates and, whether you love it or hate it, you can't escape it, so tone it down with regal purples and cobalt blues.

As we near the vernal equinox, a wave of strong colour sweeps over the garden, and it comes firstly in the form of yellow. Here gardeners' tastes divide like the Red Sea opening up before Moses: some are in the 'brighter the better' camp, and some shudder at the forsythia down the road and struggle to find their sunglasses.

I face this dilemma every year with the Best Beloved, who adores those in-your-face yellows, those bright-red tulips that open wide to reveal sooty middles, and those oversized crocuses in shades of bilious egg-yolk yellow. Worse still, he likes them all together, and I am expected to enthuse about this lurid cocktail. Interestingly, he is the introvert, the shy one who cowers in company, while I am feisty and spirited – but I still prefer subtlety. Give me cream and unsalted-butter-yellow every time.

However, this is a season when we can say 'each to their own'. Be true to your preference and don't be influenced by

gardening hype or fashion. After all, March is the month that kick-starts the gardening year, and it really is a case of planting whatever turns you on. Dark soil, emerging foliage, newly sprouting grass and well-placed evergreens flatter either type of scheme.

One plant is universal: the daffodil, or narcissus. This highly bred bulb is immensely diverse, but most thrive in cool, temperate conditions. They start into life in September (along with crocus, galanthus, muscari and scilla), and by Christmas they lie poised to flower with their buds just below the soil's surface. Temperature, not light levels, prompts their arrival, and it's quite possible to have four weeks' difference in flowering time from one spring to the next.

As a general rule, narcissi flower in an order according to colour, although there is a period in mid-April when colours overlap. The brightest yellows tend to come first, followed by the paler yellows, creams and virgin-whites. The earliest, *Narcissus* 'Rijnveld's Early Sensation', is a single-flowered clear yellow with a squat, flared trumpet. It will flower in January if planted in early September – the best time for planting all narcissus, crocus, scilla and muscari. In mild areas this variety can appear as early as Christmas Day, so it's a valuable addition to any garden. However, in cold winters it will flower later. It is a jaunty, substantial daffodil (20 centimetres/8 in.), but I have found that regular division is necessary if it is not to dwindle.

The single pheasant's eye narcissus (*N. poeticus*; see p. 48) is a native of meadows in areas from Spain to the Balkans, but it endures well in gardens and is mentioned in the herbals of the early seventeenth century. The single windmill of white, slightly twisted petals has a red-edged greenish-yellow crown at the centre, hence its common name. The double version, *N. poeticus* 'Plenus' (also known as the Tamar double white), is the latest daffodil of all to flower. It will bloom in May and is a tremendous partner for such sultry late single tulips as 'Queen of Night'. 'Plenus' produces highly scented scrolled flowers in purest white, and I have naturalized it in grass among black tulips, although it remains to be seen whether the bulbs will endure. Both single and double forms can reach 60 centimetres (2 ft), although they are often shorter.

This stretch of flowering times (from Rijnveld to pheasant's eye) covers four months, and by the time the latest ones flower the earlies are fading horribly in the ugly way that daffodils do. These withering, yellowing leaves have to be endured for a full six to eight weeks in order to allow the bulbs to replenish, although the seed heads should be removed. For this reason alone segregate your earlies from

Narcissus 'Rijnveld's Early Sensation'.

Narcissus 'Tête à Tête'.

The orange trumpet of *Narcissus* 'Jetfire' darkens to a much brighter hue as the flowers mature.

your later daffodils, at least in the garden setting, although you could get away with a mixture under an avenue of trees seen from afar. The classic combination for four weeks of flower is 'Mount Hood', a mid-April-flowering creamy white, and 'Carlton', an early-April-flowering bright-yellow of similar proportions and flower type. The two are garden stalwarts, and the slightly taller 'Mount Hood' will reach a sensible 45 centimetres (18 in.). Early daffodils need to kept away from late-flowering tulips for the same reason, but later narcissi, which tend to be pale and scented, make tasteful partners for late-flowering tulips as they coincide perfectly.

The Tamar Valley, between Devon and Cornwall, became the centre of British daffodil-growing once Brunel's Royal Albert Bridge and the Great Western Railway linked this warm area to the London flower markets in 1859. The trade concentrated on early cut flowers, for these attracted the best return financially. Three or four varieties dominated the fields back then, but they have mostly been lost or superseded.

One cut flower farmer, Alec Gray of Camborne in Cornwall, produced the most garden-friendly type of daffodil: the miniature, which is jaunty and able to resist the weather. In the late 1920s Gray began to collect seeds from the small, wild species of narcissi found in southern Spain, in the hope

Narcissus 'Mount Hood', 'Salome' and 'Sempre Avanti'.

of producing early varieties for the vase. However, the progeny turned out to be short in stature with small, delicate flowers. Although they were no good for the cut-flower trade, Gray fell in love with them and devoted the rest of his life to breeding miniature varieties.

Gray's most famous cultivar is 'Tête à Tête', which he bred in 1949. It earned its name from its habit of producing two heads per stem and many heads per bulb. This very early narcissus is long-lasting, and the golden petals and neat cups make it an excellent daffodil for the front of the border. It can also be grown in pots and is strong enough to push through grass.

Serendipity is an amazing thing, and two other well-known miniatures came from the same seed pod as 'Tête à Tête'. 'Jumblie', which was launched in 1952, is seemingly well named, for the two or sometimes three flowers are often at variance with one another. It has an uneven, random look about it. Gray named it after Edward Lear's characters, however, and not for its appearance. Its *N. cyclamineus* blood means that its deep-gold petals are swept back. 'Quince', which was launched in 1953, is the third sibling of the trio; it has soft-primrose petals and a deep cup. 'Sun Disc', another Gray narcissus, is a jonquil hybrid with straw-yellow flowers and a tiny golden cup, but it is later to flower.

Narcissus 'Jumblie' and Pulmonaria saccharata.

Another excellent variety is 'Jetfire', although at 30 centimetres (12 in.) it is technically just taller than a true miniature. This fairly new American variety has a bright-orange trumpet that is the nearest to red there is among daffodils. It is one of the finest bulbs to naturalize in grass, which is one of the easiest ways to include a range of different narcissi in your garden. Another good naturalizer is the wild daffodil lookalike 'W.P. Milner', which produces wispy pale-lemon flowers that mimic the wild daffodils of western England. The petals are swept forwards to frame the elegant trumpet as demurely as a bonnet on a Jane Austen heroine. Sprinkle bulbs by hand when planting them in grass, and try to create ribbons rather than blobs.

Narcissi are cool-season plants tempted into flower by warmth, and this makes them entirely different from the crocus, a plant that seems to respond to light and sun much more than to temperature. The narcissus is fairly happy to lurk in semi-shade, but the crocus is a sun-worshipper for an open position. The smaller-flowered forms (relatives of *C. chrysanthus* and *C. sieberi*) need excellent drainage, and produce small flowers in February and March. Fine forms include *C. sieberi* subsp. *sublimis* 'Tricolor', an early crocus brindled in purple, yellow and white, like an egg on a purple saucer. The brown-striped yellow *C. chrysanthus* 'Zwanenburg Bronze' shows up well in very early spring. *C.* 'Ladykiller' is a purple-backed white and 'Advance' (my favourite) is a warm yellow shaded with purple veins. Perhaps the most popular is the soft *C. chrysanthus* 'Cream Beauty'.

Purple and yellow are one of the dream tickets in gardening, and this contrast can be repeated throughout the seasons. Blue and yellow are equally effective together, and any bright-yellow daffodil of short stature will flatter a deep-blue hyacinth, such as *Hyacinth orientalis* 'Peter Stuyvesant' – the bluest of the blue. The dark-stemmed 'Kronos' is also excellent, as is the paler 'Blue Jacket'. This is a great combination for a container, because you can pack the bulbs in tightly for maximum eye appeal.

Winter-flowering violas in shades of blue and purple can weave a similar

Clockwise from top
left: *Crocus* 'Vanguard';
Narcissus 'Jetfire';
C. olivieri subsp. *balansae*
'Zwanenburg'; *C. sieberi*
subsp. *sublimis* 'Tricolor'.

magic with miniature yellow narcissi. Or you could use
spring-flowering *Iris reticulata*; the deep-blue *I.* 'Harmony'
and the violet-blue 'George' are both excellent in ground
and container.

The largest flowers of any crocus belong to the varieties
bred from the alpine species *Crocus vernus*. The first to flower
is appropriately named C. 'Vanguard', combining silver-
mauve petals that seem to sheathe dark-purple inners.
Collected from the wild in Russia in the 1930s, it is a star
performer in grass and at the front of a sunny border,
flowering two weeks after the smaller-flowered crocuses.

Iris 'Harmony'.

Crocus vernus 'Pickwick'.

I like to mix it in grass with three others: 'Yalta' (a smaller version of 'Vanguard'); the soft-purple *C. vernus* 'Remembrance'; and the evenly feathered purple-and-white 'Pickwick', which I prefer to the similar 'King of the Striped'. These flower up to two weeks later than 'Vanguard', and quickly form huge clumps. A tendency to bulk up is useful with crocus because squirrels are the enemy. These pesky creatures have an annoying habit of vandalizing crocus in the first weeks of the New Year, nipping off the flowering shoot from the bulb and leaving both – regardless of colour.

Excellent Additions

There are so many worthwhile plants from which to choose that I haven't been able to mention all in the preceding chapters. Here are a few more favourites to extend the planting.

Green Zing and Cool Acid-Yellow

Alchemilla mollis
The ultimate lime-green frothy plant of early summer. Common, but highly useful as long as it is not allowed to self-seed – then it becomes a thug. Cut back hard as the flowers dim. 30 centimetres/12 in.

Amaranthus caudatus 'Viridis'
Long green pony tassels from a stately annual. The perfect foil for purple and red dahlias. Does best in warm summers. 1 metre/3¼ ft.

Bupleurum griffithii 'Decor'
An easily sown branching annual, with heads of lime-green umbels held in jagged grey-green bracts in summer. 40 centimetres/16 in.

Euphorbia mellifera
An exotic, billowing euphorbia from the Azores. Produces luscious bright-green foliage and honey-scented, rust-red flowers by March, if in a sheltered position. Up to 2 metres/6 ft.

Moluccella laevis
The annual bells of Ireland, prickly and erect with spires of bell-shaped flowers in summer. Good among dark amaranths, such as *Amaranthus* 'Velvet Curtains'. 75 centimetres/2½ ft.

Nicotiana langsdorffii
Another lime-green annual, a species tobacco with tiny fluted trumpets in summer. Less prone to disease than the larger-flowered N. 'Lime Green'. 40 centimetres/16 in.

Sambucus racemosa 'Sutherland Gold'
A deciduous cut-leaved golden elder with conical heads of cream-white flowers. Lights up April and then holds its colour well. Tolerates more sun than most golden-leaved shrubs. 3 × 3 metres/10 × 10 ft.

Viburnum opulus 'Roseum'
The sterile snowball tree eventually produces white snowballs, but there's a taster of lime-green heads first, in May and early June. 4 × 4 metres/12 × 12 ft.

Cool White

Anemone × hybrida 'Honorine Jobert'
The classic white Japanese anemone, bred in 1858 yet never beaten. Round white flowers in autumn are slightly cupped to surround yellow stamens and centre, flattered by dark-green leaves and strong stems. A rambler that shifts its ground, but one that should be encouraged. 1.2 metres/4 ft.

Chamerion angustifolium 'Album'
This tall, invasive white willowherb can be planted only in certain wilder situations, but a stand along a yew hedge in a large garden is as refreshing in late summer as vanilla ice cream on a scorching day. 1.5 metres/5 ft.

Cosmos bipinnatus 'Psyche White'
This annual Mexican daisy flowers until late autumn, producing feathery green foliage and slightly double clean-white flowers. 1 metre/3¼ft.

Hydrangea paniculata 'Limelight'
The 'paniculata' hydrangeas are late-season wonders, producing conical heads in autumn. The beauty of 'Limelight' is that the colour is pure limelight: a vision of cream untainted by pink for several weeks. The heads are also a fitting size for the stems. 2.5 metres/8 ft at most.

Lathyrus latifolius 'White Pearl'
An everlasting sweet pea with racemes of clean-white flowers in July. Deadhead regularly to keep in flower and prevent unwanted seedlings. Up to 1.8 metres/6 ft.

Leucanthemella serotina
A tall, single yellow daisy that flowers from late September until November on stiff stems. A very upright plant that needs to emerge through other plants as the stems can look ragged. 1.5 metres/5 ft.

Leucanthemum × superbum 'Aglaia'
A shaggy, ostrich-feather-white perennial shasta daisy that flowers in July and keeps going until September. 1 metre/3¼ ft.

Nicotiana sylvestris
Grown as a tender annual, this tall nicotiana bears from late summer a crown of radiating white trumpets that are sweetly scented at night. 1.2 metres/4 ft.

Berry Sorbets and Good Blues

Centaurea 'Jordy'
A dark-purple form of the perennial cornflower, 'Jordy' flowers for much longer (May–September). Silver-green foliage and black, diamond-patterned buds. 45 centimetres/1½ ft.

Ceratostigma willmottianum
Small cobalt-blue flowers held in red buds make this shrubby plant a September winner. Flowers on and on. 1 metre/3¼ ft.

Clematis 'Étoile Violette'
The best viticella clematis, with single purple-blue petals set round a golden boss of stamens from July. Many more viticellas share this blue–purple–plum spectrum in the second half of summer. Cut back hard every spring. 1.8 metres/6 ft.

Geranium clarkei 'Kashmir White'
A white-flowered hardy geranium, but relevant here for its prominent purple-veined flowers in June. Good divided foliage. 60 centimetres/2 ft.

Geranium 'Purple Pillow'
A sterile geranium – so no seeds – that persists in flowering, this low-growing, compact, hardy geranium has purple saucers 2.5 centimetres (1 in.) wide, neatly veined and darkly centred, from May. 30 centimetres/12 in.

Penstemon 'Pensham Plum Jerkum'
A damson-coloured floriferous penstemon with spires of flowers from summer until autumn, if deadheaded. 1 metre/3¼ ft.

Teucrium hircanicum 'Purple Tails'
An easy and long-lived wood sage with neat tapers of purple flowers above crinkled green foliage in summer, followed by brown seed heads. Easy to grow from seed, and self-seeds moderately. 1 metre/3¼ ft.

Veronica umbrosa 'Georgia Blue'
This small veronica (introduced from Georgia by Roy Lancaster) produces excellent red foliage, and small, floppy spires of gentian-blue white-centred flowers from early spring. It does spread – although not too badly. Up to 15 centimetres/6 in.

Silver Sparkle

Dianthus 'Purple Jenny'
A small double dianthus that flowers prolifically all summer, producing plain but dazzling pink-to-purple pompoms. All dianthus need an open site and good drainage. 25 centimetres/10 in.

Geranium 'Philippe Vapelle'
Flowers just once, in June, producing cornflower-blue saucers and scalloped, softly textured green leaves. 40 centimetres/16 in.

Nepeta grandiflora 'Bramdean'
A summer bee-pleaser with larger blue flowers held in purple calices

with purple shading on the leaf. Gives a fluffier, lighter effect than N. 'Six Hills Giant'. Named after Victoria Wakefield's wonderful Hampshire garden. 75 centimetres/2½ ft.

Nepeta racemosa 'Walker's Low'
A low-growing catmint with silver-green aromatic foliage and small blue flowers in summer. 'Little Titch' is shorter and neater. Up to 50 centimetres/18 in. (Walker's Low).

Oenothera macrocarpa subsp. *incana*
The lemon saucers of evening primroses are a great addition because the clarity of colour in some is unrivalled. This silver-leaved form for summer and autumn makes a good addition to the front of the border. 15 centimetres/6 in.

Phlomis russeliana
This stiff-stemmed herbaceous phlomis produces whorls of lemon-yellow flowers in early summer and then fades to produce a brown seed head a little earlier than I'd like. It is a ground-smotherer and needs space: at least 1 square metre (10 sq. ft). It is aggressive and invades lawns. 90 centimetres/3 ft.

Salvia candelabrum
A large, shrubby salvia that's native to Spain. Royal-blue flowers with white eyes billow out on long stems for weeks in summer. A perfect partner for *Phlomis russeliana*. 1 metre/3¼ ft.

Salvia officinalis
The common culinary sage should be employed in the ornamental garden as well as the herb plot. 'Purpurascens' is stunning in hot summers, when its purple foliage takes on a damson bloom of faded velvet. 'Berggarten' is a grey-green version with larger blue flowers and rounder leaves. Take cuttings of both and cut back hard every spring. 75 centimetres/2½ ft.

Verbascum bombyciferum
A woolly white spire of lemon-yellow bells in summer that will self-seed

moderately. Its winter seed head often branches. 1 metre/3¼ ft.

Sunny Yellows, Rich Reds and Warm Oranges

Chrysanthemum 'Paul Boissier'
A hardy and easy-to-grow September-flowering chrysanthemum with rusty-orange double flowers, each with a hint of green in the middle. Up to 1 metre/3¼ ft.

Crocosmia masoniorum 'Firebird'
A very good form of this strong crocosmia, with pleated green leaves and fiery orange flowers that arch and branch from July to September. Up to 1 metre/3¼ ft.

Dahlia 'Ellen Huston'
Small, double, dusky-orange flowers – like burnt marmalade – in summer and autumn, backed by dark, bronzed foliage. A superb award-winning dahlia. 1.2 metres/4 ft.

Helenium 'Waltraut'
One of the best heleniums, with shaggy two-tone orange-and-yellow flowers from July, deepening in colour as they mature. Shorter than most. Almost 1 metre/3¼ ft.

Hemerocallis 'Stafford'
A strong day lily for July with vibrant dark-red flowers lined in white and centred with cool yellow. Stands out well in the border. 1.2 metres/4 ft.

Potentilla 'Gibson's Scarlet'
Single clear-red flowers from May onwards, set off by bright-green strawberry foliage. Fresh and lively, and excellent among ferns. 45 centimetres/1½ ft.

Potentilla 'Volcan'
My favourite potentilla, with flouncy, almost double, deep-red, long-lasting flowers in summer. Good green foliage. Difficult to find. 1 metre/3¼ ft.

Index

Page numbers in italic refer to the illustrations

First published 2011 by

Merrell Publishers Limited
81 Southwark Street
London SE1 0HX

merrellpublishers.com

British Library Cataloguing-in-Publication data:
Bourne, Val, 1950–
Colour in the garden.
1. Color in gardening. 2. Plants, Ornamental – Color. I.
Title
635.9′68-dc22

ISBN 978-1-8589-4547-7

Produced by Merrell Publishers Limited
Designed by Nicola Bailey
Project-managed by Rosanna Lewis
Indexed by Vanessa Bird

Printed and bound in China

Jacket, front: *Cosmos bipinnatus* 'Dazzler'.

Jacket, back, from top, left to right: *Narcissus poeticus*;
    Rudbeckia fulgida var. *sullivantii* 'Goldsturm'; *Kniphofia
    linearifolia*; *Cosmos bipinnatus*; *Tulipa* 'Recreado';
    Geranium ibericum; *Iris* 'Harmony'; *Muscari azureum*;
    Nicotiana 'Lime Green'.

Frontispiece: Late-season grasses, including varieties
    of *Miscanthus sinensis* and *Pennisetum*, make a great
    impact as summer moves towards autumn. They will
    sway and dance well into winter.

Page 4: The colourful borders at Great Dixter, East
    Sussex, use orange red-hot pokers and dahlias with
    dark-leaved cannas and the sultry castor oil plant
    (*Ricinus communis* 'Carmencita') for vivid colour and
    strong architectural shape.

Pages 16–17: Hybrid hellebores, pulmonarias and narcissi
    form the backbone of a spring woodland border.

Pages 50–51: Once-and-only roses capture the moment
    when summer softness peaks.

Pages 96–97: The lowering sun begins to pick up detail,
    and this dew-covered cobweb quivers, capturing the
    spirit of an autumn morning.

Pages 130–31: A mistle thrush feeds on rowan berries.

ACKNOWLEDGEMENTS

I should like to thank the whole team at Merrell,
particularly Rosanna Lewis, Nicola Bailey and Nick
Wheldon, for their thoroughly professional approach
and friendly handling of this book and me. I should
also like to thank Liz Eddison of the Garden Collection
for patiently collating the pictures.
    Finally I must thank the Best Beloved, Jolyon Kirby,
for support and help beyond the norm, and our
family (Fran, Zoe, Stuart, India, Ellie, James and Jess)
for indulging my passion so considerately over
many years.

Happy Gardening!